Hemingway and Jake
*An Extraordinary Friendship*

# Hemingway
# and Jake

## An Extraordinary Friendship

**Vernon (Jake) Klimo
and
Will Oursler**

William Charles Oursler, 1913–

DOUBLEDAY & COMPANY, INC.
GARDEN CITY, NEW YORK
1972

ISBN 0-385-02948-9
Library of Congress Catalog Card Number 72–7618
Copyright © 1972 by Vernon Klimo and Will Oursler
All Rights Reserved
Printed in the United States of America
First Edition

## Contents

II Jake and Hank

III Other Times, Other Wars

## Word from a Collaborator

Most of this book is about two men—Ernest Hemingway and Jake Klimo.

Each had a role in the story—a meaning, a purpose. Each was drawn to the other in a unique and driven way, driven by their intense individuality, their egos, their ambitions, their need to fight, to struggle with and against each other.

"Don't know if I ever mentioned it," Jake wrote to me in January 1972 aboard a freighter in Cartagena, Colombia, "but one thing I couldn't understand about him [Hemingway] was how, with all his down-to-earth thinking, he could still go along with those rich bastards that had never had to suffer as he had.

"Also, he had a certain demand for honesty, an almost fanatical desire to do the right thing, and yet here he was, asshole deep in all the rich phonies. At the same time, his real friends were Josey [Sloppy Joe], Skinner [the black bartender and bouncer], Sullivan, Charles Thompson, and Carlos [skipper on Hemingway's boat, the *Pilar*]. All real people . . .

"But I had the same real standards that he had (I think we all start with them). And I held to them. My smuggling and gunrunning, etc., had nothing to do with morals or self-deceit. I was a scoundrel and accepted it. Of course, I continued my whoring and yammering around the waterfront but *never* with any serious intentions—it was like eating a big, gorgeous meal or drinking a fine old cognac. . . ."

As the coauthor of this thoroughly unbelievable adventure story, I would like to state at the outset that these words of Jake's accurately reflect his personality and soul.

Vernon (Jake) Klimo is not one person but many. He is an eleven-year-old boy stealing rides on freight trains, filching food, and clothes, to stay alive, in various way stops across America.

He is a sailor guiding three-masted schooners across the oceans. He is a smuggler, a pirate, a blockade runner who once operated a private whorehouse in Bombay (during tie-up for harbor repairs). And whose children—four sons and a daughter—go to the finest schools. . . .

The story as Jake tells it represents the unfolding patterns of the two men chiefly involved: Hemingway, the master storyteller, and his coterie of characters drawn from life as he lived it. And Jake, a master mariner, and part of that Hemingway aura. Jake the ex-smuggler, and ex-pirate, ex-thief, and jailbird. Hemingway as Jake saw him from the fly-on-the-wall perspective. Jake—in the eyes of Hemingway, "A smart kid who just needs bustin', that's all."

The physical side, the violent side, the explosive-fists side—all this is vital. "The thing Jake had most in common with Hemingway," Jake's wife, Sandy, puts it, "is the Battered Body. Hemingway was ravaged by illness, marked by shrapnel wounds, broken bones, accident scars, and other mementos of extraordinary experience. A year or so ago, when Jake was admitted to a hospital with a fractured spine—he recovered with no outer visible signs of damage—a young attendant was assigned to take his medical history.

"The attendant began, logically, at the head and worked down, filling up both sides of the first sheet and most of the second with fractures, scars, bones, incisions, lumps, dents, misshapen digits, and various other insults. As this young attendant wrote, his face became full of dismay, wonder, and finally horror.

"After he completed the list, or thought he had, he noticed a deep scar on Jake's leg. 'What's that?' he demanded. Jake looked down. 'God damn, I almost forgot that,' Jake said. 'That's where my mother threw a carving knife at me when I was eleven.'"

Jake no longer lunges into the wild adventures that occupied so many years of his life. Today he sails great ocean-going freighters across the trade winds. In World War II, as assistant training officer for the entire United States merchant marine training program, Jake helped to equip and train tens of thousands of young seamen to handle the

Liberty and Victory ships that played a major role in winning that war.

He is married and a good father to the four sons and daughter. But Sandy still recalls the more turbulent era: "I first realized Jake wasn't an ordinary man a few days after we met," she states calmly. "We were walking down East Fourteenth Street, a car backfired, and he dropped to the pavement. None of my other boyfriends had ever done that. I learned later he had just come from a revolution in South America. . . ."

That's typical Jake. I first heard about him through my friend and neighbor on Shelter Island, New York, Captain John Russell. I am grateful to John and his wife, Lydia, for bringing Jake within our orbit.

The story this huge, powerful man tells in his own colorful words—they are equally colorful in Spanish—was tape-recorded in a number of interviews with me. My main role with Jake has been to try to draw some kind of order out of the chaos of a hundred or more stories and still not lose the warmth and flavor of his words, his meanings, and the glintings of understanding about Hemingway. And about himself.

Sandy says he is a very tender-minded and gentle man where his family is concerned, at least when life is treating him kindly. As a young man he was given to cleaning out Greenwich Village barrooms of customers who were guilty of some injustice, "like taking up too much room at the bar." When things slow down too much, he is inclined to have highly audible attacks of regret and he will say things such as, "My whole life has been wasted!" or "I haven't accomplished a damn thing in the last forty years." These remarks, along with one directed in turn to each of his four sons at around the age of twelve, "When I was your age I was hopping freights," have become stock family phrases.

I'm grateful for the aid I've had from the Russells, from Sandy, the young Klimos, and a large amount of research material, books, magazines, newspaper clippings, letters, and notes.

But this is no bibliographical story. It is Jake's story about himself and about Ernest Hemingway and the Hemingway clan as he remembers the story and lived so much of it. Let him tell it. His way.

Will Oursler

# I

# The Gulf Stream Years

## 1. Mobile Bay

That morning in the Mobile courtroom marked a real change in my life. The beginning of one, anyway. I didn't have any idea then of ever being involved with important people like the Hemingways or anybody else who counted at all. Sooner or later, somebody would bump me off. Here I was, standing before the authorities once again—the law —trying to talk my way out of serious legal trouble. And jail.

I had just turned seventeen. Six feet tall and strong. I thought I was smart enough to outwit just about the whole damned world; that was how I saw it. I'd been on my own most of the time since I was eleven; I'd ridden freight cars across tens of thousands of miles. I was big, tough, and able to fight my way out of any situation. I was afraid of nothing. I was the real, first-class gold-plated hotshot.

That was how I saw myself. That was the braggadocio kid nobody was going to knock down or keep down. To me it was all a free-swinging ball game where you made up the idiot rules as you went along.

I'd played with the organized underworld and ridden with the prohibition hoods and driven truckloads of bootleg booze in from Canada. I'd been part of a highly efficient car-stealing ring operated by a hood named Pico.

In Mobile, I'd gone into a real deal. A couple of guys and myself had gotten hold of a big tank truck—one of those forty-foot-long goliaths that deliver gasoline from the main storage depot to the roadside gas stations. It carried hundreds of gallons.

The whole thing was well planned. We got into the yard by bribing the night watchman at the gas depot. He let us in with no questions asked and we hooked up our lines, filling our truck to the top, and drove out.

Next we took the truck to a drop on the outskirts of the city—an abandoned gas station—and transferred our load to the gas station tanks. Later we'd pick up our cut from the guys we were working with.

We thought we were real smooth and smart—getting away with those hundreds of gallons of gas that easy. It never occurred to us we might get arrested.

Unfortunately, the local cops spotted us just after we'd unloaded and pulled us in. They wanted to put us away for a long time. They made chemical analyses of the gas left in the bottom of the tank car to prove it came out of that depot.

The only thing was that in court the analysis of the gas in the tank car didn't jibe with the analysis of the gas they claimed—correctly—we had stolen from the depot.

The fact was we had added a small quantity of a different type of petroleum to the residue in the bottom of the tank car. That changed the whole picture. They knew we were guilty as hell. But their case crumbled when their own analysis didn't stand up. They had to let us go.

But before they did, I had the worst tongue-lashing of my life from the judge. He picked on me particularly because I was taller and looked a lot older than the others.

I don't remember every word. But everything he said added up to one basic concept: I was a nothing; I was the all-American fuckup. That judge really ate us out. And he told me personally, "I'm giving you twenty-four hours to get out of this city. If you're found in Mobile after that, I'll throw you into the worst prison we've got for the rest of your life."

I walked out of the courtroom free—and alone. I didn't want any more of any of those guys I'd been with. I felt sick inside. The day was bright and warm but I felt like a walking dead man. I'd made a mess of my life. I'd made a failure of everything—at home, on the road, wherever it was. The world was all around me and I was seventeen years old—and dead.

There was no place to go. I couldn't go home to my family in Iowa. I didn't know where I was going that day as I walked along the Mobile Bay waterfront, that warm, beautiful morning with the harbor glittering before me— the ships, sails, cargoes, wharves.

In the back of my mind this was the one thing I wanted —the sea. I'd taken a trip with another guy down the Mississippi and learned something about sailing in what was nothing more than a big rowboat with a mast and a sail rigged up by myself.

For me, the sea itself promised things I wanted. I'd read a hell of a lot about the sea even then. Riding the freights, I'd stop in cities all over the map, and one place the cops wouldn't pick you up and boot you out of town was the public library.

Along with serious stuff—good writing—as well as some plain and fancy crap I couldn't even finish, I read about the open sea that I'd never been on. And I realized that on the sea you were cut off from all the bastards on shore—all the cheating and double-crossing and hating. It was just you and the sea and the horizon all about you as far as you could look.

I kept walking along that Mobile waterfront. Not knowing where in the goddam hell I was heading. It had to be somewhere. And I knew I had to get out of the city before they threw me into their lousy lockup.

On the outskirts of town was a boatyard, full of small boats, motorboats, yawls, ketches, sloops. I remember how the masts stood out against the blue sky. I stood looking at this place. All the gleaming hulls and boats shored up, waiting to be launched.

A fellow was working there on a small sailboat, some kind of sloop. A tall young guy about my age. He was sanding down the hull planking.

He was about the same age as I. A real lean kind of kid with sand-colored hair and pale blue eyes. He told me he had built most of this 18-foot sloop himself with the help of the boatyard people. He said he was going to put a small mizzenmast on her and turn her into a yawl.

"I'm taking her to Key West and then over to Cuba to

see my brother," he said. "Then I'll sail her across the Caribbean and down the South American coast."

"Holy Christ," I said. "That's a hell of a trip."

This big kid sure seemed confident. "She'll do it," he said. "She'll do it because I know how to handle her. My older brother—he couldn't take her across a bathtub. He doesn't know how to sail. But I do."

From his tone and look I figured there had to be some kind of conflict situation between him and the brother. I couldn't quite figure what it was. And couldn't care less.

I stood looking at that wonderful little boat and thinking what it would mean if I could only go with him on this voyage to Key West and Cuba and South America in that 18-footer.

Maybe, I was thinking, she could go around the world.

I told him I was handy with tools and rigging and I knew about boats even though I'd never been on the open sea. I could help him finish building the boat and putting on the mizzenmast.

He said that would be great; he wanted to finish the boat as quickly as possible so he could get her in the water and underway. He told me his name was Hank and I said I was Jake and we shook hands. And I pitched in, helping him to set up the rigging and the mast.

Hank kept talking about his older brother and how the brother tried to boss him and was forever finding something to carp about. That was one reason it was so important to make this trip, he said. To prove to the older brother that he could take a boat like this anywhere.

"What the hell is your brother trying to prove?" I asked Hank. "What's his goddam pitch anyway?"

"He thinks he knows everything. I want to show him, prove to him—what I can do. That's why I have to take this boat to South America."

From what I'd heard, Hank's older brother sounded like a shit. He didn't have any goddam right picking on the kid brother and driving him up the walls. I knew what it was, having people pouncing on you all the time. Telling you how lousy you were. Riding you.

That was one of the big reasons I'd run away from home in Mount Vernon, Iowa, by the time I was eleven years old. I went back there occasionally to finish my education. But I never stayed long, just in the winter. Even then, I slipped away weekends, riding freights to Wyoming or some such place.

I understood how Hank felt, but what really interested me was that trip he was planning. I asked him if he didn't need somebody to go with him, to spell him at the helm. He said he had another guy to make the run with him to Cuba. But he and I seemed to hit it off. He said if anything happened that the other guy backed out, he'd let me know.

I gave him the address of my parents' home in Iowa— from which I'd run away so many times, and returned so many times. "If anything does happen, you let me know," I told him. "I don't want any pay. I just want to go along."

Then I realized I didn't know how to get hold of him. I said, "Holy Christ, I don't have your address, Hank. I don't even know your goddam last name."

He gave me the address where he would be in Key West, Florida. And told me his name was Hemingway.

Leicester Hemingway, he said, spelling it out. But everyone called him Hank. The older brother he'd been telling me about was Ernest Hemingway, the writer.

I found it pretty funny. In all those years of dodging from one library to another, reading anything I could find on the shelves that was worthwhile reading, I never read a Hemingway book. But I knew the name, I knew it was important. How important, I didn't realize at that time.

We finished the work, and the 18-foot yawl—the *Hawkshaw*, he called her—was ready to launch. As soon as his friend arrived, Hank said, they'd sail to Key West. The next leg was over to Havana, where big brother Ernest was fishing off his 38-foot Matthews powerboat, the *Pilar* —named after a Spanish shrine. I learned later it was also a nickname Hemingway's wife Pauline used in intimate moments with her husband.

My friend Hank was heading across the gulf to the Florida Keys and Havana and South America. And I was heading for the railroad yards on the outskirts of Mobile, where I would hop a freight heading back to Iowa.

I took one last look at Hank and the boat, figuring I'd never see either of them again. I said, "Listen, you bastard, if you want me on that trip with you to Havana—let me know. I'll be home in Mount Vernon, Iowa. Waiting."

He grinned and waved his hand.

## 2.  Big Blue

*As it turned out, I was wrong. I did get a telegram from Hank Hemingway informing me that his friend had conked out on the trip from Key West to Cuba. Could I make it to Key West?*

*Three weeks later I was in Key West staying at the Ernest Hemingway home with Hank and his sister-in-law, Pauline, who was Hemingway's wife at the time. There were also an ebb and flow of assorted friends, relatives, and domestics.*

*Two weeks after that, Hank and I were in Havana Harbor, living on the 18-footer and anchored about fifty feet from where Ernest Hemingway was living on his famous boat, the* Pilar.

*I've jumped over a lot of goddam stuff because I wanted to get to where the action starts—and that means Havana. Maybe I'll tell some of that other stuff later. I'm not following any special historical chronology.*

*This one happened weeks—or maybe months—after*

*Hank and I arrived in Cuba. It concerned a big blue marlin Ernest Hemingway had to have—the biggest blue ever pulled out of those Gulf Stream waters.*

*It also concerned a moment of triumph and profound meaning for several of us on board the* Pilar.

Incidentally, we called Hemingway "Stein." This was long before anyone called him Papa. Stein was the name we called him inside the family circle. He used to invent nicknames for everybody. And Stein was short for the nickname he called himself: Hemingstein. Somebody said it stood for beer steins. He drank a lot of beer.

Stein was very competitive. And he hated this guy Zane Grey. I was an overgrown eighteen-year-old when I was first down there and I didn't understand all this competitive business. I thought the reason Stein hated Grey so much was because of the writing side of it and Grey's zooming success.

Grey was right at the peak of his fame. He'd made all the dough he could spend after *Riders of the Purple Sage* was such a big smash seller, and he made a bundle in Hollywood besides. I thought that was what was bugging Stein. But it wasn't. The real reason had to do with fish. It was because Grey had been going around winning all the prizes in big-game fishing, especially blue marlin. Grey had retired and bought himself a big power cruiser and gone all over the damn ocean breaking records for game fish.

The *Pilar* was one of the old Wheelers—a beautiful 38-footer with Chrysler engines that went for about ten grand even in those days. Stein was out to break Grey's record for blue marlin in the Caribbean. He really meant it, too. It was like something obsessed him.

I remember he used to say, "No wonder the son-of-a-bitch has got the record. He fishes with clothesline."

Somebody else would call out, "Aw, Stein, you know better than that."

And Stein would answer, "Yeah, I know. But I can think it, can't I?"

He was after that record. And we were out with him, helping on the boat, Hank Hemingway and I. He was after the record for blue marlin and nothing else at that time. Nothing else, not his writing, not anything mattered, in that period. Weather permitting, we were out in the stream every day.

It got to be a grueling, driving thing for all of us. You got swept up in it. Fishing every day, hunting, hunting marlin. We got so we thought it, ate it, slept it. Nothing was good enough unless it was the big one, the really big one that would smash Grey's record. He had to have the biggest blue marlin in the whole goddam ocean. Day after day we'd be out there in that dark blue stream, riding the stream, trolling, watching, listening, waiting. Stein was like a haunted person much of the time; you could see it in the hard glitter in his eyes. The truth was—I decided later—he was like one of his own characters in a story.

For one example, his character Harry Morgan, in *To Have and Have Not*, describes a moment fighting for a marlin: "Then I saw him coming from behind under water. You could see his fins out wide like purple wings and the purple stripes across the brown. He came on like a submarine and his top fin came out and you could see it slice the water. Then he came right behind the bait and his spear came out too, sort of wagging, clean out of the water. . . ."

This fish, this marlin, was something Harry Morgan needed, and Ernest Hemingway needed. It was something each had to have, like dope, like a woman in bed. It was a crazy thing.

Throughout the days and weeks of that hunt on the *Pilar* there was Stein and there was Hank, his kid brother, and me. For the rest, it would vary with who was down to visit us. Of course, there was Carlos, the skipper, a little *Gallego*—from Galicia, Spain. The *Gallegos* are the earthy people of Spain. The term is also used for the hard-working, unimaginative people who do the work, the drudgery jobs that have to be done and nobody wants to do. You could sell a *Gallego* the Brooklyn Bridge—he'd believe you and buy it and then he would try to take it home.

Stein hired Carlos because he was the best blue-marlin fisherman in the world. He'd been skippering big fishing schooners out of Havana, but his primary thing was blue marlin. This man even looked like a marlin. He had a long nose. I claim he thought like a marlin. That's what we called him—*Aguja*, the needle. The marlin has a long nose, like a needle.

This man Stein hired as skipper of the *Pilar* could smell marlin if they were anywhere around the boat. He'd talk to them, he'd call them my children's bread—*pan de mis hijos*. He'd talk to that big fish like a friend, he'd honey it in, one word at a time, one turn at a time. Carlos and Stein would talk and argue and curse at each other about how to bring it in, and Stein would call, "Jesus Christ,

13

you *Gallego*—you thick-headed *Gallego* son-of-a-bitch. You do what I tell you." And Carlos would say in Spanish, "Listen, you're so big and stupid, you don't know how to bring in a fish. You don't know how to handle a fish. . . ."

The tension of the sea hunt grew. All of us felt it. It would be hours trolling out in the stream, fighting to capture the one that had to break the record. We took a lot of fish in those weeks. Each one was a battle. The *Pilar* was outfitted for that kind of job; she had three fishing chairs in the stern area. These were the fighting chairs.

To start with, we'd put out two trolling lines about a hundred yards out, each with big pieces of cero mackerel on them. Then you put out two teasers—they're just feathers—about fifty feet behind the stern to attract the marlins. When the goddam marlin moved in he'd come up astern of the mackerel. You could see this big sail of the fish come up—my God, it was a frightening thing to see that whole great sail of the big fish emerge out of the water.

Then he would follow the mackerel, and eventually, if he was sure, he would hit it—he'd hit it with this bill of his, this *aguja* of his. At that exact moment you have to let go of your drag so that it looks as if the marlin has stunned the mackerel. If you keep the drag on and the mackerel bait keeps going along on a taut line, pulling away from the marlin, he'll know right away something is wrong. He hit that thing and it should have died, it should have stopped dead. Something's wrong.

You have to let the drag out, let it go loose so the mackerel bait seems to stop. Then the marlin takes the mackerel

14

bait; he'll take it in his mouth and he'll turn and swim away. Now, he'll get a certain distance and he'll swallow that bait if you let him. In that case, all you can do is strike him and kill him that way; you'll be pulling out his guts. You've taken him but it isn't fair; it isn't sportsmanship in the terms of the real hunters of big-game fish.

It has to be in his mouth; you strike him then, at just the precise moment when you feel sure he has it, but before he swallows it. You can be sure there is much shouting and cursing and advice in moments like that. And they're yelling, "*All right . . . strike him, he'll swallow the son-of-a-bitch if you don't strike him . . .*" You wait. You wait for that explosive moment, with the boat moving and rolling in those surging Gulf Stream swells.

Then you hit him. . . .

For more than a month, day after day, we were out hunting for the fish that would give Stein the record. It remained an obsession he could only be rid of by fulfilling its demands. We caught fish, all sizes of fish, from small ones to big, but Stein kept on after *the* big one. At night we would drink and argue and fight the whole battle over again.

It became a virtual ritual, the getting ready for the day, the setting out, the struggle for a real strike, and the going back in for beer or heavier booze, for arguing, especially between Stein and Carlos. And the next day was a brand-new fucking ball game.

But the day came finally when we did land the big one. Stein made the strike and Stein fought it and ultimately, in that long desperate struggle, Stein won.

This is an overwhelming, running, jumping, diving, plunging battle, the fish leaping for its life, this high twisting form dancing on the tips of the waves. The blue marlin is a tremendous creature. The sea is his domain and he knows it and uses it well. The odds are all in his favor. Most of the time, especially with amateur fishermen, he'll get away. This time Stein was there to win.

For more than an hour and a half, Stein played this giant; leap by leap, foot by foot, he brought him in, gaffed him, brought him aboard the boat. For Stein it was the hour of challenge, as important as any in his life, his work, his writing, anything. His enemy, his antagonist, was there—more than a quarter of a ton of powerful, magnificent, fighting fish.

They fought the desperate battle, these two, at either end of the line, one for its life, the other for the game and the glory. It was Stein who ultimately won—who had to win. Stein had broken the record for blue marlin in the waters off Havana.

Stein had a suite in Havana's Ambos Mundos Hotel. The name means "two worlds." Word of his victory spread quickly, and people began coming up to the suite to celebrate. Bullfighters, actors, writers, friends, pilots, officials, everybody who could squeeze in. It was one of the greatest drinking bashes in the history of the city.

Anyone who was anybody was there. But among them were a lot of other types—fishermen, shrimp-boat captains, jobless people, broke people, obscure, unknown people who were also his friends. It was a wild hassle. Everybody wanted to be with Hemingway in his momentous hour of victory over a big blue fish.

16

That marlin was all Stein was thinking about—that and his sweet victory. Nothing else counted that afternoon, that night. Not for Stein, not for any of the scores of celebrities and others who jammed in. It was the everybodies and the nobodies, as Hank Hemingway put it. No one minded or cared; no one heard what anyone else was saying.

The big blue marlin was all Havana was talking about that night. And, of course, everybody, or almost everybody at least, got drunk.

The party wore on into the night. At last people began drifting on home. There were good-nights and congratulations, and limousines and taxis were waiting outside while bartenders and waiters kept bringing in more drinks and ice and carting off the empties.

It kept on like that for hours, until after two-thirty in the morning. . . .

There were just a handful of us left. Stein's close friend, John Dos Passos, was there, but he wasn't drinking. Stein was there, of course; it was his night, all the way. And I.

Stein was still all wound up in the fish, still excited and obviously not ready for bed. I was young and full of piss and I could drink booze like water. Stein obviously had to keep going. So he said, "Jesus Christ, let's get out of here. Let's get down to the *Pilar* and spin some yarns. I've got some special Spanish wine I've been saving on board. Come on, let's go."

All the others had drifted off, various couples had shacked up. Hank Hemingway was out cold. Dos Passos, Stein, and I went on down to the *Pilar*. We got out to the

17

boat and began stumbling around on the deck in the dark and woke up Carlos, the skipper. Carlos was angry at being awakened this way at this hour. "Tomorrow," he said, "we go fishing again. What are you doing here, waking me up this way, stomping around the deck?"

Stein said, "For Christ's sake, don't you realize what it means, you old mule? I broke the record. I set a new record, didn't I? Don't we have a right to celebrate? Come on, Carlos, break out the wine."

So Carlos got out the wine and we went out on the after-deck, where the fishing chairs were, opened up the wine and poured it into glasses and drank a toast to the victory and the blue marlin that helped make it. Stein, who was leaning back in one of the fighting chairs, announced that we would make like Boccaccio. "We're all here together. Each of us has a chance . . . each of us tells his story. Any story he wants to tell."

Carlos and I were over on the starboard side of the boat. Carlos said in a low voice in Spanish to me, "Who the hell is this Boccaccio? Is it something like *Borracho?*" *Borracho* means a drunk.

I said, "No. Boccaccio was a guy who wrote and told stories hundreds of years ago. A bunch of guys were caught in an old tavern in Spain or Italy and had to spend the night, so each had to spin a yarn . . ."

"Why?" Carlos demanded. "What did they do that for?"

"Why, to kill the night. Just the way we're doing now."

Carlos thought a moment. He looked up at the stars. Then he said, "Si, si. You tell the stories. I'll drink the wine."

It was late. The lights along the shores and the docks

18

were mostly darkened. There was only a gentle breeze moving the boat slightly as she turned on the anchor.

And Stein, sipping the glass of wine occasionally as he sat in the fishing chair, began to tell the first story.

### 3. "Carlos, . . . Tell Us About a Fish . . ."

I had never heard it before, and I'm sure none of the others on the *Pilar* that night had ever heard it either.

Stein had wounded a Cape buffalo in Africa and was trailing this wounded buffalo through the elephant grass. Once you've wounded an animal like that, Stein explained, you have to kill it, because if you don't, if you leave it, the animal will either die in agony or it will attack and kill any unsuspecting guy that happens across its path. This Cape buffalo, Stein explained, is the only animal he knew that had the quality of revenge. Once you've wounded one, you'd better kill the bastard, because he will get you, even if he has to wait days to do it.

"I had to get it," he told us. "I was in the elephant grass trailing the buffalo. I was sure it was somewhere ahead of me. But I couldn't smell it. The Cape buffalo has a real strong smell you can't mistake."

Stein added, "I quit smoking, because it interfered with

my sense of smell. I wanted to be able to smell and taste and touch everything." The reason for this was that he was almost blind. Without his glasses he couldn't see. He had to have those glasses. That was one of the things, I had discovered, that piqued him. He was working half blind most of the time.

And smell was important in this story. It was life or death. "Because I was trailing this buffalo," Stein said, "and the wind shifted and I smelled that god-damned buffalo behind me. In other words, the buffalo had circled fast and now it was trailing me."

"The whole situation suddenly reversed. A moment before I was the hunter—now this buffalo was stalking me. Now I was the hunted. I ducked off the trail into the tall grass. I was standing, waiting. And here comes this big Cape buffalo, covered with blood, sniffing along the trail, following the scent."

And the way Stein told it—Jesus, the hair stood right up on your head.

The way he described this big monster coming in and trailing him. And if the wind hadn't shifted and he hadn't smelled that buffalo—they do stink, full of ticks and everything else—Stein would have had no chance whatever. The buffalo would have killed him.

There, on the *Pilar,* that night, Stein depicted his own feeling vividly, the sense of surprise at the sudden reversal of their situations and the growing horror—the dripping, the oozing blood from this critically wounded colossus, whose one last reason for living was to destroy the man who sought to destroy him.

"Suddenly, everything had changed, everything had

21

turned around," Stein said, "including my own feelings and emotions, now that I, and not the Cape buffalo, was the one to be hunted down. Suddenly I was thinking like an animal myself, where to turn or hide or stand before him.

"Luck had been with me. A man has to have luck. Life hangs on it sometimes. If the wind had not shifted, that animal would have come up behind me without any warning and trampled me to death.

"As it was, the wind shift alerted me and I took cover. As the buffalo came close, I raised the gun and took dead aim. I finished him with a single shot."

That was Ernest Hemingway's yarn as he told it on the *Pilar*. I had never heard it before and never read it in any of his writings, before or after that time. I kept looking for it, too. I always wondered why somewhere he never used that experience in his writings.

I can never forget, either, that it was part of that night, part of the excitement. Nor will I forget Stein's words, in that clipped, husky way he had of talking, as he built the horror of the moment of vengeance and death.

There was a silence on the *Pilar* after Stein's story. Carlos refilled our glasses with the wine. Stein looked up, saw me, and said, "Okay, Jake. You're on."

I'd been in Havana with him long enough by then to know that Stein insisted on truth; you had to talk about what you knew, never what you didn't know. I told a story about myself as a runaway kid; and about a boy who wanted to be a star athlete in high school, but who wanted to go hoboing with me for experience.

22

I explained how I rode freights all over the country, lived with hobos and bums in the jungles, and stayed away from home sometimes for months at a time.

"Home," I explained to the others, "was Mount Vernon, Iowa, on the main railroad trunk line crossing America. I didn't know much about this boy who wanted to go along, or what he wanted to be, except that apparently he'd gotten the notion that he wanted to go on this freight-train ride the way I was doing. We rode the freights for a couple of months and, coming back to Mount Vernon, we were on a steep and dangerous grade. We wanted to get off but I realized how damned dangerous it was and I told the other guy I wouldn't jump. He wouldn't listen to me and jumped anyway.

"At the time, I didn't realize that anything had gone wrong. We'd been gone quite a ways and stopped a number of times. At one of the stops, another fellow who'd been riding in another freight car on the train told me the kid hadn't made it: When he tried to get off, his leg went under the train and the wheel cut off his foot. The yard bulls—police—took the guy to a hospital.

"I thought I was pretty tough; I'd seen and done everything you could do, practically. But this thing about the boy's foot bothered me. I hadn't been part of getting that kid on the train or off it. But I knew him and I had a feeling of responsibility. I had to do something about it.

"I felt this strongly and urgently. I said to the fellow who'd told me about it on the freight, 'What did they do with that boy's foot?'

"He looked at me like I was crazy. 'What did they do with it? How the hell would I know? Probably chucked it

23

in the ash can or just left it. Who cares about the goddam thing?"

"I knew I had to do something. It seemed to me terribly important. I had to go back and find that boy's foot and bring it to him. I felt somehow responsible even though I wasn't.

"At the next junction, I got off and hopped another freight heading the other way—back to where my friend had gotten off. Sure enough, in the bushes by the tracks where the freight had slowed, I found the foot. And I wrapped it in newspaper and took it up to the hospital where they'd taken him and gave it to him."

I explained that I never could understand why I thought he had to have that foot, but it was very important to me that he did; it was his and I carried it up there to him.

I said, "I'm older now—maybe I understand a little more. Because that kid had heard about me hopping freights and I was sure that gave him the idea. This boy had always been the best athlete in the high school and had dreamed of being the star football kicker on the high school team.

"I learned afterwards that he went just about nuts because of his lost foot and I agreed to help him somehow. The next vacation from school, he and I went on a canoe trip down the Mississippi, all the way to the mouth of the river. It took us the whole damn summer. One thing he could do, with or without a foot, was paddle a canoe. And I rigged up the mast and a sail. It was a hell of a trip.

"Neither of us had any money. We had to live by our wits. I wanted it that way for a lot of reasons, but mostly because he had to learn that he could take care of himself, could live by his own efforts. That was part of what I wanted him to see.

"Filching a bottle of milk off the front porch or a loaf of fresh bread, or stealing fish out of holding traps farmers set along the river banks—that was how we lived. Only, you have to do it late at night—not when those farmers are sitting back in the bushes somewhere waiting with a shotgun.

"It was a bastard of a trip. The river has a hell of a current, especially for a boat that size. It took us three long goddam months. But that boy who lost the foot was grateful, really grateful. He said it was the greatest trip he'd ever had in his whole life."

That gave us a story of violence in the African jungle and a blood-and-guts story of a kid's foot. And then it was Dos Passos, who sat beside Stein, his face almost hidden in the shifting harbor night shadows. Dos told a wholly different kind of story. It was a charming thing, unlike the others in character and equally unlike the abrasive reality in depth one usually associates with Dos Passos.

It took place while he was attending the traditional Run of the Bulls over the ancient paving blocks of the village of Pamplona, Spain. Along with this highly publicized festival through the narrow streets, there was dancing and laughter and wine flowing free and unrestrained. Visitors and natives alike were half blind on the local booze.

"I was as loaded as all the others," Dos admitted. "Why not? This was the time, what better time could there ever be? When I finally turned in, it was about three in the morning. I hardly remember hitting the pillow.

"When I finally awoke, or came to, or whatever you might call it, it was obviously late: the sun was well up and the maid was cleaning the room. I assumed she decided that she had to get her work done, and since I was obviously out cold, what did it matter? The truth was I was just emerging from this self-inflicted coma. I could just barely open one eye.

"Through that one eye, however, I could see this Spanish cleaning maid, her hips and backside jiggling in the morning sun. This girl really had it. And I was looking at it, you know, trying very hard through this single opened eye.

"Then she turned around and she has this low-cut décolleté maid's costume as she moved about the room with her duster, paying no attention to me whatsoever. It was really very disturbing, the whole thing. I was lying there helpless, and all I wanted to do was to get up and get hold of this seductive maid's round breasts and that round rump flitting about the room in front of me."

And then, he said, came the most frustrating, agonizing part of all. "I knew I couldn't get hold of her. I couldn't get out of the bed, in the state I was in, after those gallons of wine. Worst of all—I couldn't even open the other eye.

"I lay there, watching her through my one available eye. Unable to raise a hand. Or anything else. I was helpless. And there she was so close, so palpably available. And so unreachable."

Usually, I had discovered, Dos Passos talked quite fast, occasionally stumbling as though his words could not keep up with the rapidity of his thoughts. But at that moment, it seemed to me he slowed up as he recalled this episode of feverish immobility.

"I could still see her moving about the room. Once or twice she glanced my way. I couldn't speak. I tried to smile. Then she was picking up mop and broom and towels. I heard the door close behind her and her footsteps going down the corridor to the next room."

We were all pleased at this delightful story with its overtones of regret and frustration at anything so near—and so far.

Stein, who was now enjoying himself thoroughly, turned to Carlos and said, "Carlos, now it's your turn."

Carlos said, "Look, I don't know anything about this bullshit stuff. Cape buffalo, freight trains. And Dos in bed with a maid. I don't know things like that."

He didn't want to tell a story. Stein kept at him a little and Carlos was saying, "No, I am no expert on anything like that. I can't tell you anything like that. What do I know?"

And Stein, who was usually arguing with Carlos about something anyway, said, "Listen, you old bastard. You know fish, don't you? You know fish better than any other human being alive. Tell us about a fish, Carlos."

## 4. The Boy and the Sea

When he was thirteen years old, Carlos said, there was a terrible depression in Cuba. Everybody was poor, everybody except the very rich, and no one had enough to eat.

"We were a big family and we were poor and most of the time we were hungry," Carlos was saying.

It was what they called, in Spanish, "the time of the skinny cow," meaning economic depression. There was starvation or near-starvation like a blight across all Cuba. This was about two decades before the crash of 1929.

"We were starving like everybody," Carlos said. "And I had seen these big marlins they'd bring into the harbor; only the poor couldn't buy them, because the poor had no money. And I thought, like any thirteen-year-old, that I had to do something myself, I had to save them. And I could do it by bringing in one of those huge fish.

"So I borrowed a 17-foot rowboat that had a little mast, a thin upright stick for the mast, and I started out of

Havana Harbor fishing for marlin. I was outside in the stream in this small boat and got my sail up and I was trolling. I don't know how long it was—hours it was. And then—Holy Father, *Santa María*—a big blue marlin came along and hooked my bait. That marlin—it was the biggest thing I'd ever seen in all my thirteen years of life.

"I held on to it. I wasn't going to let it go. It was flesh, it was life, it was food for me, for my parents, my brothers and sisters. For three days and three nights I fought that fish. I didn't know where I was. That fish pulled me and that boat something like forty miles off the coast, forty miles out to sea.

"It was a terrible fight for a boy that age. I had fished in the stream before many times, but I had never done anything like that before. It was a true life-and-death struggle for me and the fish, for everybody. And after all that, finally I won. Finally I beat that great hulking thing and I brought him alongside my boat and I tied him on. It was longer than the boat itself, much longer."

By this time in his narration, Carlos was highly excited in his mind and memories and words, and he was jumping about the stern and gesturing and acting out, on the after-deck of our boat, this pitched struggle he had gone through on another boat years before.

"That son-of-a-bitch of a fish was mine; now it was our food for the winter. And I started back in my boat with its precious cargo tied on.

"It was then that the sharks began to come. They moved in all around the boat, scavengers tearing away at this great prize I had taken. Lunging at this fish, closing in and moving out of reach, but always staying close by, dorsal

29

fins moving with the boat, relentless and always there, day or night, moving in to tear at the fish.

"I tried to fight them off with every possible weapon. Nothing on board would stop them. I broke my oars trying to beat them off; I broke the mast. They just kept on with this silent assault, tearing away, eating away the fish, hour after hour as I tried to keep the boat moving back to the harbor. In the end there was nothing left but the head, the tail, and the skeleton."

Carlos was about forty years old at that time, and as he told that story, as he reached back to that moment of what to him and his family was real tragedy, he cried. He had been reliving the whole thing all over again, spearing the fish, playing the fish, all of it. And he was saying, "My God—my God! There was enough meat on that fish to feed my family the whole winter. And those goddam sharks got it all!"

When he got back to port with the boat and the skeleton, he didn't even have strength enough to pull the boat up on the beach. He just stumbled out and flopped in the sand. "And my grandfather came down and saw me," Carlos said, "and he picked me up and carried me home."

All of us agreed that his story was the best.

I thought about that story many times over the years. A thirteen-year-old boy fighting the biggest marlin Havana had ever seen—in a rowboat. Fighting it for three days and nights alone. No fighting chairs, no heavy lines, no one to help with the gaff.

About a quarter of a century later, my wife was reading

*Life* magazine and she called out to me, very excited, "Jake—here's Carlos' story."

I said, "What do you mean?"

"You remember," she said. "You told me about the kid who caught the big fish."

"Oh, yeah. Sure."

She says, "Well, Hemingway wrote it."

And she gives me the magazine.

Well, when I looked at it I said, "My God—it's twenty years since I heard that story with Carlos telling it that night, partly in his pidgin English, partly in Spanish."

And then I sat down with the magazine and read his tremendous story, "The Old Man and the Sea." I thought, how interesting that he made it not a thirteen-year-old boy, as it had been in real life, but changed it to an old man, an old man who failed. As indeed the thirteen-year-old boy had failed. But the boy would have time to recover. For the old man it was different.

It was more interesting, I thought, Stein's way. And deeper. Because the way Stein makes it, the old man is you and you and me. And you're not going to make it; nobody makes it. You'll fight like hell, but you're always going to lose; for each of us, in one way or another, this is the way it is. I wondered how much of Stein himself was the old man, fighting the marlin, fighting and winning, but ultimately losing.

That was what it was saying, in effect. And I thought how moving that story was. And true.

## 5. A Character Out of a Book

People down there in Havana and Key West used to ask me about myself and my background and how a guy like me happened to find himself part of the Hemingway inner circle. And I think it's important here for people to understand.

If I believed in destiny or fate or any such crap, which I don't, I'd almost think that was the kind of force that drew me to Hemingway. I myself might be considered pretty much a 100 per cent piss-poor uncivilized Hemingway character, straight out of one of the stories. I didn't plan it that way; that was how it worked out.

Mount Vernon, Iowa, where I was born, has a population of one thousand. My father was the stationmaster, my mother a schoolteacher. They'd met when they were both living in the same boarding house in Onslow, Iowa. He was a telegrapher then.

Telegraphers were bigwigs in those days. They could

always get work, anywhere they went. I think my mother married my father because she figured they would be moving around a lot. It turned out he was a man who loved home and family and hated traveling anywhere. They had a hell of a marriage.

I never got on well with my mother; she had a way of trying to run everybody's life. We were brought up by edict. By eleven years old, each of us was supposed to decide what he wanted to be. By fourteen, our careers, whatever they were, had to be actually launched.

I thought this whole thing was crazy. I loved my father and loved being around that railroad station and the tracks and engines. I knew the trains and schedules and switches like my own fingers. One day I was playing around, practicing with the telegrapher's key. My father saw me, and he said, "Listen, son. Let me tell you something. Railroads are finished as big time. Don't go into them. . . ."

The truth was, I didn't have an idea in hell of what I wanted to be. I was nine years old.

My brother John always wanted to be a musician. At eleven he agreed to be a symphony orchestra bass violinist and, backed by mother's goading, got himself apprenticed at fourteen to the chief bass violinist of the Chicago Symphony—with the promise that they would make him the best bass violinist in the world. He may not have become best in the world, but he became one of the three men in the world so gifted they performed solo at highest concert levels on the bass violin.

Jimmy, my second-oldest brother, also went along with mother's program. At eleven he announced that he would go into art and sculpture. He began almost at once studying

33

art in Minneapolis, and later he got to work on the great stone faces of the Presidents at Mt. Rushmore, under the direction of sculptor Gutzon Borglum.

When I was eleven they said, "What are you going to do?"

What was I going to do? How in hell would I know at that age what I wanted to do for the rest of my life?

I looked up at them and I said, "Hell, I'm going fishing."

The truth was that my mother's overwhelming ambition had put on too much pressure in my case.

She wanted all her children to be tremendous successes, famous and rich, so that we would fulfill what she had not been able to achieve herself. Two of my brothers were already on the way. They were successes already. And I was the failure. That was how I saw it. I decided the only thing to do was to clear out. I'd been raised in the freight yards. I knew all about them. When and where and how you could get on or off. Where and how tramps and hobos lived.

One morning, before dawn, I walked down to the yards, alone and on my own, and climbed aboard a freight.

I was gone about a year. I traveled across the country in assorted boxcars. I learned to handle myself. I learned not to say too much, not to talk, not to be the fresh kid. Old-timers on the freights and in the jungles, hobos and tramps and drifters—these were my teachers.

With them I was an equal, accepted for whatever I was. At home I was a misfit. I remember my brothers used to say, "All right, now, make up your mind. What are you going to be?"

And I would think: *What am I going to be? Except to be what I am. To learn to live, to see the world, to drink it in, all of it.*

34

And I would answer, "Okay. I'll be a cowboy."

They said, "Then you'd be nurse to a horse."

I said, "Okay. I'll be an aviator."

They said, "That's the same as being a truck driver. An airborne truck driver."

It seemed to be, even at that age, that my life was a lost cause. I had failed multiplication tables in the third grade and they put me back a year. This put a lot of doubts in my mind about myself. Anyway, I wasn't happy in school; I had a block of fear about mathematics.

Back then, at eleven years old, I was sure I was a stupe. I learned later that my I.Q. test was high. But in those days I worried that maybe I had a screw loose.

So I ran, not from the world but into it. I lived with people who didn't know me but who accepted me. I learned to steal, to pick up milk bottles off a front porch in the early dawn and a loaf of bread left in front of a village grocery. I was arrested a number of times. I was in a lot of jails. Usually I managed to talk myself back to freedom.

One cell I was in, a former inmate had scrawled on the wall: "This cell has 3421 rivets in the walls and ceiling." With nothing to do, I started counting—and came out with the wrong answer. I counted twice more; each time the result was different.

Then I realized that son-of-a-bitch had done the same thing. He knew I'd get a different answer each time, just as he had. Undoubtedly he thought it was a hell of a joke.

I stopped counting and went to sleep.

The ride on my first freight took me from Mount Vernon east to Clinton, Iowa, on the Mississippi River. From Clinton I rode another freight, which went back west right through my home town. I remember thinking as we went by, "So long, home town. I'm on my way."

I had in mind going to Wyoming. When I was younger I had been out there with my mother on the cattle ranches where they had the longhorn steers. They were spooky, dangerous, like wild cattle. A longhorn steer is really a wild bastard.

Finally, I got to Cheyenne, stayed a day or two, and went back to riding the rails. It took a while even to get that far. You had to watch out for railroad police, yard bulls and dicks. Being that young, I had to hide all the time. Mostly I traveled at night and hid in the hobo "jungles" during the day. You were pretty safe usually in the jungles.

City authorities sometimes came in and would shoot up a jungle and put holes through the pots and pans and the huts. Then the cops would come and the heat would be on and everybody would duck for cover.

The jungles were full of kids running away from home. If you were always smarting off, they'd larrup the hell out of you. Give them intelligent answers, keep your mouth shut the rest of the time, and be halfway pleasant, and some old-timer would take you aside and teach you the ropes.

*Where're you running from, kid? Trouble? No trouble . . . Nothing . . . Just like to travel . . . Listen, was it the home . . . you couldn't stand home? . . . That wasn't it. They weren't bad . . . They're fine people. I was the one . . . I wasn't good enough . . .*

You learned never to ask questions, never ask a man about himself, never ask him his name, even. To this day I can never ask a man his name. Figure out a name and give it to him; you give him the name you think he ought to have.

A lot of them were underworld figures. A lot of them were like me—hiding by day, running by night. They kept to themselves, didn't usually talk much. Loners stayed on the edge of the jungle, and as they talked to you, if they did talk, they were always watching, looking this way or that.

You had to learn about the trains, how to get off before it pulled into a station or yard, and get back on when it pulled out on the other side of town. You had to learn which freights were carrying what. "Hotshot" trains, such as the gold trains carrying bullion, also carried an armed guard in every car. They'd kill anybody trying to get on.

I made a mistake once and got on a silk train—silk was big in those days. When I climbed on, I found myself looking down the barrel of a shotgun. The guard said to me, "Jump, kid. Jump." At that point the train was rolling like all hell. I told him, "I can't—I'll kill myself if I jump."

The guard lifted the gun and said, "If you don't jump, I'm going to kill you right here."

I jumped—rolling down the bank and tearing the skin and flesh off my arms and thighs. Otherwise I was unharmed.

The railroad people themselves, conductors and brakemen, were kind men. I've had a brakeman come along and spot me and say, "Hey, pull in your goddam rump—there's a dick behind me." Or I've had them say, "Hey, kid. This is Missoula, Montana, we're coming into. Be sure to get off before we're in the station. This is a real tough place if the bulls spot you."

I've had them help me plenty, the railroad men—me, a punk kid.

But I learned.

In the jungles, I studied the men. I began to notice the bigmouths and the stupid ones and the ones that made sense. Listening and analyzing the differences in the way they talked, I began to grasp that what made the real difference was that some had education and some hadn't. You could tell by their mannerisms and talk and thinking. I decided I had to go to school. Six months later I went back to Mount Vernon to go to school.

It was a big confrontation. All the questions. Where've you been? Why? My mother's brother had done the same thing I did—only, he stayed away twenty years. That fact had scared the hell out of my mother. They were mighty relieved to see me.

My old man said it must have been tough out there. I said, yeah, it was sure good to be home. They decided the only thing to do was to leave me alone, let me do what I wanted, do it my way. That was the best thing they ever did. I studied in summer school and went back to school in the fall and made up for all the lost time.

Every weekend and every vacation I disappeared, and they never asked questions, before or after. And I was all over the map. It was El Paso or the Rockies. Or Seattle. Or back up north to Milwaukee. Mostly I stayed out of the East because of the big cities. I'd work my way south, west, and midwest. Came Christmas vacation, and three days later I'd be in the deep South. By the time I was seventeen I'd had a double education . . . one in school, the other in life. I was fully grown, over six feet, and weighed a hundred and eighty. I could get drinks, and I hired out to follow the harvests and I worked in shipyards and on road gangs.

One night, up in northern Minnesota, a guy and a girl gave me a lift in a big limousine. The guy gave me a drink of prohibition booze in the car and suggested I stay at his motel—they called them cabins in those days.

I stayed there that night and I woke up with one hell of a hangover. The guy who gave me the lift came in and he said, "Why don't you stay here awhile?" As it turned out, he was fighting with the girl and wanted to throw her out and go down to Minneapolis and get another one. He said he wanted to leave someone there he could trust while he was gone. And I'll be from here to hell if he didn't leave me to run the camp.

It turned out to be a drop for bootleggers bringing in stuff from Canada. The little guys would come up to the motel to pick the stuff up. I was given a pistol and left in total charge. As he left, he gave me the keys and said, "You take it, Jake. I'm going." I had a cook, a woman that cleaned up the joint, and a handyman.

The guy from Minneapolis never showed up again. Every time stuff came in and went out, I got money. I took my just share, that was all. Nothing else. But I was beginning to taste the world. Life. Big time. God damn dangerous, but exciting as hell. I headed back to school that year with a lot of cash, just a little over five thousand dollars. And a handsome pair of golf shoes they had for sale in the front office.

That's how I got in with the crowd and in with that guy stealing cars and gasoline down in Mobile.

## 6. Open Seas

All apart from the verbal reaming I got from that judge, Mobile itself was no vestal virgin. I did some pro and semi-pro boxing there myself, fighting prelims at five bucks a night, won most of them, but several times came near having the living shit beaten out of me.

I didn't give an aboriginal damn if I never saw the place again.

After my meeting with Hank Hemingway in the boat-yard, I hopped a freight heading north and west and wound up in Mount Vernon four days later. All I was hoping was that I'd hear from Hank that he needed me on that cruise to Cuba. I worried the mails and pestered the telegraph office. Nothing happened. A week went by, two weeks. I was getting fidgety. Then, about the end of the second week, came this telegram from Hank telling me the guy who was going to Cuba with him had dropped out. Could I make it soon to Key West?

I got down there as quickly as I could reasonably make it—riding this time in a passenger train, with a paid ticket, for the first time in my life. For about the first time in my life also, my parents—especially my mother—seemed to have some respect for what they considered their washout son. I was moving up with this Hemingway thing. Maybe I wasn't a total loss, after all.

I joined up with Hank at the Hemingway home in Key West. The house was a Spanish-style dwelling with windows that went from ceiling to floor. Draperies and shadows and sun. Pauline and the boys were there—this was Pauline Pfeiffer, Stein's second wife. She was a charming hostess, gracious and reserved, but with a real piquant sense of humor. Once, in the midst of some banter, she said, "Hank, you getting all you need? All the loving you need?"

Hank looked startled and stuttered some answer and Pauline said, "Well, I'd help you out myself—if I weren't married to your older brother."

It was so-called froth and frivolity. People coming and going in the semiurban society of the Key West world. Some years older than I was, Pauline treated me with the pleasant informality of the place and the time. I was the house guest of her husband's kid brother.

We stayed there that first time only a few days. Once, wandering alone around the Key West main drag, I ran into an old friend—Pico, the big-shot Cajun who ran the car-stealing ring up in Mobile. He was delighted to see me. He was getting into something new, he told me. Bringing in Chinese aliens from Cuba. Maybe I'd be interested, he said.

I shrugged. I said, maybe someday I might.

But all I really cared about right then was getting out on the water in Hank Hemingway's 18-foot yawl and sailing her to Cuba.

Ten o'clock at night, a couple of days later, we said our good-bys to Pauline and the boys and got underway.

It was the first time I'd ever been on the open sea, the first time I'd felt the wind hit my face, as we cleared the harbor and headed into the waves and the swells.

This was an experience I could never forget. It was like a dream, the lights in the Key West harbor, the flashing red and green and white marker lights along the shore, and the brightness and nearness of the stars.

We split watches, four on and four off—you had to take the tiller the entire four hours. Hank had the helm down the channel heading out from Key West. The only instrument we had on board was one small compass. When we finally got outside the harbor, into the open sea, Hank handed the helm over to me. All he said was, "You take the watch, Jake. Steer two twenty-five magnetic."

And he went below to the cabin and went to sleep. It was the first time I'd ever taken the helm in open water. I got the tiller and began moving it around and learning how to handle the helm in a boat this small. Our pint-sized yawl was jumping and twisting and plunging around like an eel on a hook. I wasn't the least bit scared by this. I didn't care what it did. I was having the time of my life. I was afraid of nothing. I was looking up at all those stars, at the whole damn lit-up sky, and I thought, "Holy Christ, this is where I belong, where I've always belonged."

I was at the tiller most of the time alone—we took turns sleeping down in that cabin. It was rugged going, really pretty strenuous—a little boat like that jumping around in the swells.

We hit the Gulf Stream just about dawn after the first night. When Hank woke up he said he was looking to hit it pretty quick—he'd been kicking around out there alone in the days he was waiting for me to get down there.

That was a real moment, coming into the stream. The line when you hit the stream is a sharp demarcation—the stream itself is the deepest blue I have ever seen. The dawn light was like a mirror—pink-white light that shimmered in the blue water. The gulf weed—sargassum—was brown against the dark water, and the white foam blown in the wind was about the most beautiful thing I'd ever seen. It was the happiest moment I'd ever known, that moment, beating my way in this plunging little yawl from Key West across to Havana.

Here, in this vessel, after years of running and waiting and wanting, years of being of no value to anything or anyone, I found what I wanted. I was steering a sailing ship—a yawl—across these seas. I was part of something—legitimately. All these years of nothing—from eleven to eighteen—reached a bloom and a blossom in this trip.

The squall hit us late the next afternoon. I was below when it hit, and I remember being batted around in the cabin. I hurried up to see what was happening. We were running into nasty waves—foam and whitecaps—and sharp winds, and we dropped the mainsail and shortened the mizzen and the jib. She was pitching and rolling in that

43

wind, and the lashing on the jib got loose and it started crawling up the forestay. Hank called to me across the wind, "That jib's got to be brought in, Jake." He started forward, but I called back to him, "I'll get it, I'll get it. Don't worry."

It was no easy thing to do in the storm. I crawled out along the deck, clinging to the rigging, and finally managed to straddle the bowsprit, and I hung on there somehow and fought the jib down. I don't know how I survived. The boat was like a spinning top, twisting, diving, heeling in the water. When she plunged, the sea would come up to my waist as I sat astride the bowsprit like a kid on a rocking horse. The sea was foaming but the water was warm. I hung on with my legs while I was fighting the sail. The yawl would go way up clear of the sea, and then plummet down like she was bent on total destruction.

I still had no fear of any of it. I don't know why. I suppose it was all the other experiences, years of riding freights, jumping on and off, hanging onto a coupling between cars, working with hoods and bootleggers. Nothing fazed me at that age.

It took us four days to make that ninety-mile crossing. Half of the time we were hove to in the cabin riding out the winds and mountainous swells. We were driven some forty miles east of Havana, carried by the winds and the Gulf Stream.

When we first caught sight of land and we could see the tops of those mountains on the Cuban coast—we were a good many miles off—I caught the odor (the wind was blowing offshore) and I smelled for the first time that smell of the tropics, the sweet blend of fruits, tobacco, roast coffee, heat and palms and sea.

We headed toward shore and came into a little cove, where we spotted a fisherman in a boat. Hank asked him in Spanish which way Havana was. The Cuban pointed west. We had charts, but they were unclear, short on information and detail, and there was nothing along the shore itself to give us a clue to where we were.

The next day we spotted a lighthouse and identified it on the chart. We were abeam of Mantanzas Bay. We sailed all that day and night, heading back toward Havana, trying to make up the miles we'd been driven off course by the storm.

Late the next afternoon I saw a big cruiser coming at us, a big powerboat, running at top speed and cutting a big swath through the water, bearing down directly on us. As it came closer I saw this guy—to me he was all glasses and mustache and pearly teeth—waving a bottle of beer at us. And looking just like a twin brother of Teddy Roosevelt.

But it wasn't Roosevelt. It was Hemingway, Ernest Hemingway, grinning and waving and shouting at us as he brought the big Wheeler cruiser up alongside and tossed us a couple of bottles of cold Cuban beer—Hatuey Beer, it was called, after a Cuban Indian chief.

And he says, "Come on. I'll give you a tow."

I looked over at this guy grinning and laughing at us and I thought he doesn't look like a bad guy, after all. I knew he must have been scared that we'd been lost making that run. It should have taken us only two days at most, but with those winds and squalls it had taken four. Stein had been out there in the *Pilar* hunting up and down that coast, looking for us.

We were only about two hours outside of Havana Harbor

when Stein came up with the Wheeler and took us in tow. All the way back in he was whooping and hollering and throwing us bottles of that cold beer. I'll never forget it. Hank hadn't handled much liquor, but I'd been drinking from my earliest days. I knew how to handle it. Hank was pretty high on beer by the time we got in.

Inside the harbor, they anchored and we anchored, and after we were squared away on the yawl, Hank and I dove in and swam over to the *Pilar*. I climbed aboard and walked over to our host, held out my hand, and said, "My name's Klimo."

He grinned, shook my hand, and said, "My name's Hemingway."

I said, "God damn, thanks for the beer. That was really good—tastes like Bohemian beer."

Stein laughed. He stood there talking to me about the trip over and how crazy he thought Hank and I were to cross from Key West in a boat that size. "That's no boat for the open water," he said. I was trying to figure him out. I'd already formed the opinion, from all I'd heard, that this guy was a prick. I also knew Hank was in awe of him. And belligerent about him.

He was real, that much I knew, flesh-and-blood real; he couldn't be anything else. I resented this big son-of-a-bitch giving his kid brother a hard time. But I was thinking, hell, he is what he is.

When we got over to the *Pilar,* all kinds of newspaper people and cameramen began coming on board to interview us and get the story of how Hemingway rescued his

46

kid brother and pal, meaning me. They swarmed all over the *Pilar* and all over the *Hawkshaw*.

It was pretty exciting and exhilarating, flash bulbs popping and look over here and look over there, and we want you by the mast with Hank and Ernest and how the devil did you guys dare to come over in a boat this small? All the way across the straits. Hell, it can get rough out there.

The reporters kept asking questions, mostly, of course, of Ernest Hemingway. But the fact that our boat was the smallest sailboat ever to make the crossing to Havana from Key West to that date was also news.

For myself, all I wanted to do in that little boat was keep on going. All the way to South America. And from there— maybe east to Africa.

It all made a huge splash, with big headlines on the front pages the next day, and pictures of all of us and all the details about Ernest Hemingway's saving his younger brother and pal in the Gulf Stream.

The only thing I remember made me sore—they spelled my name wrong in the papers.

## 7. The Gold and the Dross

I used to spend evenings with Dos Passos, who wasn't well and didn't get around too much, whether we were in Havana or up in Key West. Dos was one of Stein's closest friends down there, but Dos wasn't well enough to go out every night boozing it up with Hemingway and the crowd at all the bars. And I didn't have any dough for that kind of stuff. So we used to spend some of the evenings together.

Dos never talked about his writing, but he talked about other things. He was studying insects, for example, to beat hell. He told me the insects would take over sooner or later. His theory was that they were far more organized than humans and we were so disorganized as a world it would be a cinch for them to wipe out humanity. That was before someone thought up DDT.

Dos was a strange guy. As usual, when he did talk, he talked very fast; it was almost a stammer. I had the distinct idea once in a while that he resented talking because he had said it already in his mind.

He liked me a lot. For one thing, he had to take pills regularly. I didn't know what the trouble was, and naturally, didn't ask. But he had to take pills at a certain time, and if he went to sleep, which he sometimes did, especially after a drink or two, he might miss the designated time. So I stayed with him, talking some, but mostly listening. And I'd wake him if he happened to doze off before he had his pills.

All the gang around Stein took that attitude. They were always there to help if needed. They were quite a group—celebrities, non-celebrities, would-be gatecrashers, painters, and poets. And a changing pattern of people out of the group he had known abroad, particularly in Paris.

One was a guy named Canby Chambers, who was there in Key West with his wife. Canby was always the life of the party. Usually pretty well oiled up. He was a polio victim, with zero use of his lower limbs, and had to be in a wheelchair wherever he went. But he had developed his torso and his shoulders until they were massive and powerful.

Canby had a strong, handsome face, and he was really impressive, even in that wheelchair. He had been a part of the group Stein knew in the Paris days. As a matter of fact, Canby insisted he'd been more broke than all the rest of them. It had been harder for him, too, because he couldn't walk.

But he was a writer, and he knew he had to sell something somewhere, and when the good stuff he wrote kept coming back, he turned to writing penny dreadfuls—cheap, shabby, penny-a-line fiction. I remember seeing some of his stuff running under his by-line in an English newspaper. They used it right on the front page.

Canby liked to go out carousing a lot of the time with Stein, whooping it up in various joints and bars. I didn't have the dough to keep up with that crowd—I had virtually no money at all.

I didn't even have pin money, actually. Hank used to spot it every once in a while and he'd slip me a fin or so and I didn't like that. I didn't like it at all. I don't like charity; I wanted no part of it. I'd rather be a thief, if I had to, to stay alive.

Hank would argue, "Oh, come on, Jake. You're helping me with the boat, aren't you? You're helping me sail her, aren't you?"

And I'd say, "Don't give me that shit. You're trying to put it on a salary basis. You couldn't pay me a salary. I'd either go with you or I wouldn't."

This was the writing world, the literati, sophisticated, successful people who later would be called "the beautiful people" for want of a better term. I wasn't either a writer or successful at anything. Yet they let me be part of this world.

Hank would go out on the town; he had to be in it, especially if Stein was there. I didn't care. I'd spend the time back in the hotel room with Dos.

One night Canby Chambers wasn't feeling well, and he said, "Hey, Jake, if I stay here will you feed me pills, too?"

I said sure, why not? He said, "I want to stay with you and Dos. To hell with that party the rest of them are going to. I'm hung over."

Behind his words I felt there was something else. He didn't like to go in public, because he had to be in the wheelchair all the time. They'd do the rounds and they'd all be dancing and he couldn't make it.

But I remember Canby especially that night he stayed with Dos and me, because he got stewed and told a story. His own story about himself.

Canby said they were with Stein in Paris in the days when their whole crowd was starving and Canby and his wife, Esther, starved along with them.

He and Esther lived together in a typical left-bank flat, where the crowd would drop in sometimes. And Canby and his wife discovered that when these people came they would surreptitiously leave something behind—a carton of cigarettes or a bottle of wine, a loaf of bread, small items they would seemingly forget to take along as they left.

They wouldn't give it to him; they'd just leave it. That was a time when Canby was trying to write the great book, the great novel, really serious literature. And he was starving. Nothing he wrote sold, and they all knew it and were leaving these items of food and wine. That, for a guy in a wheelchair, just didn't go down too well. Canby told Dos and me, "I had to do something. I couldn't just sit there. And I couldn't go out and get a job, either. That was when I began hacking, when I started writing this horrible crap, this shit I couldn't stomach myself. But I wrote it. It sold and sold and I kept writing and writing, pouring it out. And the checks were coming in and by God—I was a success."

I remember Canby giving me a funny look when he said that. I understood why. A couple of weeks before that, I'd

51

told him that I thought of myself as a failure—all my past life—up until the time I got with Hank and these people.

"So, basically because of the carefully staged forgetfulness of my Parisian pals," Canby went on, "I got down to writing and selling and making enough money to eat and something more. That was good—even if the stuff itself was adulterated crap."

Canby paused. Then he said, "It was dreadful. I had money. But now I was dead as a writer, as a real, creative writer.

"And then came the miracle. The absolutely unlooked-for miracle. I was making enough now for all our needs and more. But it was Esther who pulled the real switch. Esther inherited a cool million dollars. Just like that.

"The situation had totally changed. We had all the money we would need for the rest of our lives. I told Esther, 'Now I don't have to write this stuff any more. This dreadful crap. Now I can write what I want and what I've always wanted.' And Esther agreed completely.

"I began to write my novel. And serious short fiction. Only nothing happened; nothing came out of the typewriter worth a shit. The words simply were not there. I had all the great ideas, and the time and money I needed to write them. And I couldn't write it. Not a line. Not a god damn line I could sell."

You could see the terrible frustration in Canby's handsome face. He turned to me. He said, "Jake, let me tell you something. You're young enough to listen. I won't try to tell Dos anything—I can't tell Dos anything. But I want to tell you and you can tell anybody else you meet who wants to write, that if you want to write something, write it well, or don't write it at all."

I remember the long pause in the room. Dos said nothing; he was just sitting there listening. He had said nothing through the whole story. I was really shocked by the urgency with which Canby said those words to me.

Canby's eyes were burning into me. "Don't ever write hack, Jake," he said. "Don't ever write shit. If you do, you'll wind up exactly like me."

"Now what do we do?" he asked. His whole tone changed. "Nothing. Sit out on the beach in the morning, get a little sun. Every afternoon I get gently drunk; I get loaded. That's all there is to it. I don't have to hack any more. Esther's got a million bucks."

## 8. Fists in the Afternoon

I was big and hefty, like Stein. I'd fought in the ring and could handle myself; I was young and afraid of nothing. Essentially I was the physical creature, just as Stein was. He lived and wrote the world of five senses, of violence, body contact, blood, bullfights, prize rings.

I was twenty years younger than Ernest Hemingway. And when he told me to put on the gloves and go a few rounds with him—as he did on a great many occasions, usually after siesta time—it wasn't only because he wanted, as he put it, to knock some of the oven-baked bullshit out of me. It was also true I presented a challenge. A twenty-year-younger challenge.

Boxing was a test for me, too. Stein was big, tough, and even at his age he was strong as a bull. I wanted to knock him down, to show him my alleged cockiness wasn't just words. I felt I could fit into anything—any group, any situation—anytime. But I was always in a hurry; I moved

like the wind. I had to make it quick, I had to get my dukes
on a load of money quick. Later I found that every time
I'd get my mitts on a wad of dough, I'd try to parlay it
into something bigger, and Jesus Christ, what am I doing
but going right back into hock again. I kept asking myself:
Where the hell is any of this getting me?

Part of it, I figured, was what Stein recognized as young
bullshit. Part of it was something in me and in himself,
too: a slugging, two-fisted response that had to be sub-
dued.

So we'd box in the afternoon, Stein and I.

Every afternoon we'd anchor for a rest—we'd troll all
morning, and about noon or just after, we'd stop and cook
and have lunch and beer and take a siesta. Then, around
three o'clock we'd box.

Often we'd box out on the afterdeck of the *Pilar*, which
was wide enough and big enough. It was all open; it had
no overhead.

This was no patty-cake exhibit; it was battering, and at
times almost brutal. We were exchanging solid clouts to
body and face with all the strength we had. No punches
pulled. Years later, I came to understand something about
Stein's affinity for the bullfight and the prize ring. There
was a streak of the bullfighter in Stein himself, a kinship
between his fists and the matador's sword.

To me it was amazing that this man, who was virtually
half blind, could still box. I finally figured it out after boxing with him for months. Like the bull—and the matador,
too—Stein waited for movement. If you stayed perfectly

55

still, he would have to rush you to make you move so that he could see movement.

He'd rush hell out of you, swarm all over you with those hard, pummeling blows. You had to have a real good defense or a terrific offense, the way he'd rush you. Man, he was powerful. He knew he was a good fighter, too, a hell of a fighter. He laid me low, god damn; he was ruthless in the ring. There was no playing around. When you put on those gloves, you went in there to fight.

I never knocked him down. I wanted to like all hell. We traded a lot of hard punches and I landed as good as I took, but I never succeeded in knocking him down. He had me down three or five times anyway. And I came out of some of those sessions with cuts or bruises or welts. Nothing fatal.

The truth is that this bruising drive was a part of Stein's basic character; the sudden vicious clout was part of his being in his writing and in his life. It was his explosive reality.

He lived by his own rules. He never carried money, for example. Mostly, he had a buck or two in his pocket. Sometimes not even that. Money didn't mean anything to him; he let other people handle it; he spent it fast, he got rid of it.

On one occasion he bought a big dinner for us at the Ambos Mundos Hotel. One of his wife's friends was there —a rich bastard. Stein didn't like him; he considered him an overbearing son-of-a-bitch. Among other faults, the guy didn't know anything about game fishing and refused to take any advice from anyone who did.

Anyway, this guy was at the party. When it was over,

Stein, as usual, signed the chit, but you had to tip the waiters in cash. Stein reached into his pocket and said, "Oh, Christ—I haven't any cash to tip the waiters." He turned to a friend of his and said, "Give me a ten; that ought to take care of them."

The friend gave Stein the ten-spot, and Stein put it on the plate and told the waiter, "This is for all the waiters."

But Pauline's friend had been watching all this, and the moment he put down the ten-dollar bill, the guy came over and put down two tens on top of Stein's.

Everybody else was talking or milling around, getting ready to leave; only one or two of us were watching this by-play. Stein saw it, of course. His expression didn't even change. He simply picked up the guy's two tens and handed them back to him and said, "Here's your money."

Then, so fast you could hardly see it, Stein's fist came up. The two were standing very close; the blow itself didn't carry more than six inches. It was a short, hard, crushing smash to the guy's jaw. A straight one to the jaw.

The guy went backward about three feet. The wall saved him or he would have gone down. He was so startled as he crashed into the wall he didn't even drop the two tens. Stein turned and walked out.

His meaning was clear. The guy thought the tip was too small and he had the money to throw around. It was his way of trying to show Hemingway up. He couldn't show Stein up on the boat; he couldn't do it fishing. He wasn't big enough or fisherman enough. He thought he could do it with his two ten-dollar bills. But he couldn't.

Of course, there was hell to pay, because this was one of Pauline's close friends. It was the kind of clash that could

57

really break up marriages, especially involving an ego like Stein's. Pauline was even then trying desperately to make the marriage go, but it was slipping. She knew. After all, she had stolen him from Haddie Richardson, her college roommate, who was Hemingway's first wife and his first love. Pauline was only losing what she'd stolen anyhow.

Stein had ego and vanity about his public image. I read a column by Leonard Lyons years later in which he recalled an incident at the Stork Club, in New York City, when, according to the column, a man at Lyons' own table accosted Stein at another table, and flicked a few mock blows at him without landing any. The third time he did this, Stein hit the guy and knocked him on his silly ass.

At the time this incident occurred, the late Dixie Tighe, of the New York *Post*, wrote a front-page story with a different version. She claimed the guy came up to Stein and said, "So you're the tough Ernest Hemingway? Let's see how tough you are." And with that he threw a punch at Hemingway, which missed as Stein turned away from this nut.

Lyons' tag line to his own item declared, "Although I was at the table and had witnessed the proceedings, Miss Tighe's version was the one Hemingway believed."

More likely, I would guess, it was what he wanted the world to believe. Basically, inside, for all his four-letter words, Stein was a prude.

Yet, the more I knew him, watched him, studied him, the more I realized Stein was not only a hell of a fighter, he was also a hell of a human being, with a hell of a sense of humor.

You saw that side in small things. He loved to laugh, to tell stories. He mingled. He abhorred the phoney, he rejected the bore. He accepted the obscure individual on his own terms.

One boxing incident involved a situation where Stein found himself overmatched. I was the one he seemed to like to clout most, but he boxed some of the others in our inner circle also. Everybody had to get in a lick or two. At one session, Stein's oldest son, Jack—Stein called him Bumby—was on hand to watch the fisticuffs. Stein and I had been going at it pretty hard, pounding the hell out of each other.

Bumby was then about seven or eight years old and seemed to be getting a whale of a kick out of all this. Finally, when we knocked off, Bumby asked his father, "Can I fight you, Poppa?"

"You want to fight me?" Stein asked. "Yes, sure. Why not?"

So they got all set, in this father-son confrontation, and Stein got down on his knees and they started fighting. Stein still had on the gloves, but he let Bumby fight without gloves, bare-fisted. Stein was sparring, playing with him, but Bumby wasn't swinging very hard, not hard enough for Stein, anyway. Stein says, "Come on, Bumby, come on. Hit me. Really hit me hard. Larrup the hell out of me."

Bumby decided to follow his old man's instructions. He reared back and unwound with one that got Stein right on the goddam nose. It was really a good one, and Stein wasn't looking for it, and it got him flush in the face.

That was a lalapalooza. Stein's eyes ran and his nose

swelled up and it was bleeding. Bumby saw what he'd done to his father and he started crying. Stein was sitting there looking at Bumby and laughing. But he was concerned also that Bumby was so upset and he said, "It's all right, Bumby. It's nothing."

But Bumby said, "No, no—the blood, the blood."

And Stein told him, "Aw, a little blood from a nose-bleed. There's nothing to worry about. Nothing at all. Anyway, I told you to hit like that. And you did what I said. You did just fine."

And he sat there, holding his son and laughing, blood still trickling down from his swollen nose.

## 9. A Knife in the Dark

The knife was one of those sudden, unlooked-for episodes you could find yourself in with Stein. Hank and I were living on the yawl and getting our food and booze aboard the *Pilar*. The drinking usually started anywhere between four and five in the afternoon. Mostly they served daiquiris— dozens of daiquiris. Gallons of the stuff.

Life in Havana Harbor was extremely informal. Nobody dressed for dinner. Stein was usually barefooted and in shorts during the day—at night he would dress up to the extent of putting on a shirt. Hank and I would swim over for meals and socializing.

In those days, pleasure boats and sailing yachts didn't raft up to each other side by side the way yachtsmen have come to do since. In Havana Harbor, yachts rode at their own anchors. No moorings were available, and the word marina hadn't even been invented.

You never knew who might drop over to visit on the

*Pilar* in the early evening; it had to be people Stein knew or wanted or had invited; it might be a famous artist or a visiting Frenchman Stein had known abroad. More often than not, it was some obscure individual whom Stein had taken an interest in or liking to. No one should forget that Stein belonged with and loved the so-called small people, the nobodies, much more than he did the big shots and the pushers.

The night of the knife, Hank and I swam over to the *Pilar* and I had with me a wonderful new possession of which I was inordinately proud—a brand-new knife I had bought myself that day—at a bargain price—in the Havana market place.

This was a beautiful knife. The blade was long and thin and delicate and finely honed. Most knives you get in the United States have a thick blade that may be all right for hunting purposes, but they are no good for sailing or cutting knots or lines on a boat. The best sheath knife on a sailing ship is a long slender blade; then you can get an edge that slices cleanly and quickly rather than wedging and sawing its cut across the fibers.

On any ship—a sailing vessel especially—when you have to cut a rope it is usually to save your life, and you may not have five seconds to lose.

The knife I bought was a beauty. The thinness of the blade was exactly right for my purposes; the heft was beautifully balanced. I was proud of this new possession. On the *Pilar* that night, I was showing the new knife to some of the guests. I was talking with one young guy who asked about how did you defend yourself if somebody came at you with a knife. Well, I'd never been in a real knife fight, but I had seen one or two in the various hobo jungles and backstreet slums. I was giving this guy the benefit of my knowledge, such as it was.

Stein was on the other side of the boat, talking with three or four people. I didn't realize he was paying any attention to me at all. In my exuberance I was giving this guy a running demonstration of how to block a man coming at you with a knife.

All of a sudden Stein turns, leaves the people he's with, and comes over to me. "No," he booms out. "No, Jake, for Christ's sake, you've got it wrong. You've got it all wrong."

I was holding this knife in my hand and looking at him. I said, "What do you mean, Stein?"

"God damn it," he said, "you couldn't hold off a man with a knife that way. You'd be dead." Then he half grinned and said, "Come at me with that knife, Jake. I'll show you what I mean."

Other people on the boat noticed something was happening, and they were watching. There was a sudden hush. Everybody wanted to know what was going on.

The afterdeck was lighted up—that was so people wouldn't stumble around or fall overboard. Stein was waiting for me to lunge at him with the knife. He was in shorts and sneakers—he hadn't even bothered to put on a shirt that night. And he says, "All right, come on. Come at me with the knife."

I started at him, holding the knife high, and made a half-looping swing I knew he could block easily. If I had made a mistake I could have killed him. Stein roared out, "Not like that, for Christ's sake, Jake. I said come at me with the knife. I mean it. Come at me hard."

I thought to myself, all right, here goes. He's got to block me, he's got to block that blade. So I reared back, and this time I went at him with the blade coming down as hard as I knew how to swing.

Stein chopped. It was a quick chop, like a karate chop, with the side of the palm. Short and hard and fast as greased guts. I hardly saw it, hardly knew it was coming.

That incredible chop did the job Stein wanted to demonstrate, ostensibly for my benefit. The knife spun out of my hand, over the side, and into the dark harbor waters. This was my knife, my precious possession, and I wanted it. I could see it starting to sink and I leaned way over trying to reach it and was almost ready to dive for it—I could swim a long way under water and was ready to dive to the bottom if I had to—but Stein came up behind me and grabbed me by the belt of my trunks.

"You god-damned idiot," he said. "Don't you ever do that." And as he pulled me back he gave me a real hard chop on the head.

"But, Stein—the knife. It's my knife; I want to get it back."

"You want to be eaten alive, Jake?"

"Of course not. But I . . ."

"Listen," he said. "This harbor is full of moray eels. They're dangerous as hell anytime, but especially at night. They're extremely dangerous. Don't ever dive into the harbor this late at night. They could kill you."

Swimming over to our boat was one thing, Stein also

pointed out. Diving down to the bottom for a knife in that water at night was suicide.

Later, he seemed to soften a little. He'd hit me with the chop to the head and he'd cost me the knife, and he said, "God damn it, Jake. You ought to know better."

About an hour after that, he came over and offered me a drink, which was a special thing. Usually the normal thing was, if you wanted it, you went and got it. But this time he was trying to soothe my ruffled feelings. And later that night we got drunk together and sat out there talking on the deck. Most of it loaded talk, half-drunk talk.

I would like to say that the next morning there was a brand-new knife by my breakfast plate on the *Pilar*. But there wasn't. Stein undoubtedly figured if I was stupid enough not to hang onto that knife, it was my fault, not his.

## 10. The Lady on the *Pilar*

During this period in Havana—with the *Hawkshaw* anchored close to the *Pilar*, we usually had dinner with Stein and whoever else happened to be aboard. Booze was there for the taking. You helped yourself like everyone else. It was unfettered, easy living, Hemingway's days and nights in Havana Harbor.

But there are moments when an eighteen-year-old kid brother and his pal can be, as the French term has it, *de trop*.

A few days after we got there, we were aboard the *Pilar* and Stein says, "You guys don't know Havana, do you?" And he turned to me and said, "You ever been to Havana before, Jake?"

I told him, no, I'd been to Canada and Mexico and every state in the Union, but that this was the first time I'd ever been outside the continental limits.

He began warning us about the dangers. "This is a real

tough time down here," he said. "There's a first-class revolution cooking and there could be bombs and shooting and people getting killed."

It was just about the time that the insurgent party had ousted Machado, and Batista had taken over the government and was going about cleaning out pockets of resistance and making sure he was firmly entrenched. There were strikes and opposition protests and killing and terror.

Stein said he was giving us a guide named Choo-Choo, who knew the city well and would give us a real rundown on the joint and what was what. Hank and I were looking for real excitement, and this so-called pilot was lugging us all over the map to see cathedrals and the ancient fort, stuff neither of us gave a shit about.

What we wanted—or I wanted, anyway—was the danger, the waterfront, the dames, the dives. Hank as much as I, actually. This was the first time he had been away from home, so we were straining at the leash. It was pretty thoughtful of Stein to go to the trouble of getting us a guide. Stein knew the place was filthy with disease and pimps and dope peddlers and all kinds of pretty raunchy stuff.

So we didn't stay too long touring the city with Stein's so-called pilot. Most of the time we were on our boat, out fishing with Stein on the *Pilar* while he was after that big marlin, or swimming over for breakfast or dinner on Stein's boat.

The trouble was that Stein—with his wife, Pauline, back in Key West with his sons—had begun playing around with a gal.

During this period of the lady on the *Pilar,* life changed

67

for the whole entourage around Stein. Stein himself had changed, for one thing, while she was there. He had a different attitude, an air of happiness; a deep, personal thing you could tell in the man. There was a fresh gentleness in his manner; the barb, the sharp cutting-you-down-to-size comment was hardly in evidence. He was a rugged man—but a gentle lover. And he was allowing himself to enjoy the episode the way a kid savors a bar of candy.

One change was that dinners on the *Pilar* didn't last long into the night the way they had when she wasn't there. There weren't many people dropping in. Nothing was said openly, of course, but everybody knew. Soon after dinner was over, Hank and I—and any other visitors on board—would leave. The night under the stars above the *Pilar* belonged exclusively to Stein and his lady.

Fortunately, or unfortunately, Pauline, back in Key West, got word of what was going on. Aware that her marriage was in serious trouble, she was still unwilling to surrender without a battle. She packed up her boys and herself, came over on the ferry to Havana, and went out immediately to the *Pilar*. The lady already had departed. So had Stein's aura of happiness. The adventure was over.

Later that day, around cocktail time, Hank and I swam over to the *Pilar*. We didn't know what had happened or that Pauline had shown up with the boys. The moment we got there, I realized what was going on. Stein, looking thoroughly miserable, was reading a newspaper and saying nothing; Pauline sat on a deck chair some feet away, knitting. The air was thick with their emotions, Hemingway's and Pauline's, tied up in their terrible silence.

It was anything but a happy moment, and no time for us

to be there. I got the message right away. Maybe because I'd seen a lot and done a lot. Hank simply didn't catch on, didn't really know what was happening. He was yammering away about the pilot character Stein had gotten for us, saying something about how that goddam Choo-Choo was nothing but a pain in the backside, or words to that effect.

Hank didn't realize what Stein was thinking and feeling. He kept on about this stupid Choo-Choo episode. Stein jumped up, threw down his paper, and said, "You dumb son-of-a-bitch—I paid good money to have that guy show you around Havana and save your stupid ass and you stand around bawling me out about it." He was really in a rage as he talked, and actually drew back his fist and was about to let his kid brother have one.

Just at the last second, he drew back his fist and didn't go through with the punch.

Pauline sat there knitting, not saying one word.

Hank still hadn't caught on and looked at Stein as if he was crazy or something and said, "What did I say, Stein? What'd I say that was so awful?"

Hemingway said, "Aw, just keep your mouth shut, and when somebody does you a favor don't knock it to hell like a piece of shit."

Pauline listened but went on calmly knitting in silence. She knew what was really happening—her husband was taking it out on his kid brother instead of her. The blow he was almost ready to throw at Hank was the one he really wanted to cut loose on her.

It seems almost as if Pauline was the wife in "The Snows of Kilimanjaro," the rich wife who uses her money consciously or otherwise to destroy the artist. That's the way it

69

has always seemed to me, and that was how it seemed to me that night, long before the short story was written.

Her family owned Richard Hudnut perfumes, and her old man was in politics and owned half of Arkansas. She was used to easy spending money. While the husband is sitting there dying of a gangrenous leg in Africa, the wife sits calmly beside him, not really able to reach him or even sympathize with him, or understand why he felt that marrying a rich woman had wrecked him as a writer.

When I first read this story I thought it was one of the best goddam things Stein ever wrote and I knew whom he was writing about—in almost all his characters there were elements of people I knew, including this man dying of gangrene and going into delirium and cursing his rich-bitch wife who had all the money and had ruined him as a writer with that money. It was Stein's projection of Stein.

It is possible that the story about becoming a hack that Canby told Dos and me could have been a secondary source for the story. Stein must have heard it—from Canby himself or Dos Passos. But the episode with the lady on the *Pilar*, and its bitter marital aftermath, were almost certainly the basic source.

Canby was only mildly bitter about himself. There was no deep tragedy there. It was all too late, it was all decided in his case. It happened and he accepted it. But Harry, the dying husband in "Kilimanjaro," did not accept it. As Hemingway, living, did not accept it either. What died was Pauline's marriage.

Still, the image of Pauline seated off by herself, quietly, wordlessly knitting, was the bitter substance for the story her husband, Stein, would make world famous.

A few minutes after the outburst, Hank and I swam back to our own boat. When we were turning in, Hank said, "Jesus, he's unreasonable. I didn't say anything and he almost took a swing at me."

I said, "Hank, don't you realize what's happening? Here the air's all charged up because he's been caught playing hanky-panky and she comes rushing over here to protect her interests. They probably had a terrible fight already over that woman."

Hank knew all about the affair his brother was having—or had been having. He simply hadn't realized that Pauline knew also and that was why she was there. I said, "Sure. You walked in with your big fat feet and you made one remark and he blows up at you. The one he really wanted to hit was Pauline, Hank, not you. You were just a convenient substitute punching bag and he almost let you have it. If I'd have said something—anything—he'd have swung on me, too."

Hank turned out the light in the cabin and went to sleep. It was late now in the harbor. The two boats were quiet and dark—Hank and I in our boat, Pauline and Stein and the boys in the other.

## 11. Brothers

I could see how deep was the rivalry between Hank and Stein. Hank was the younger; the burden of the rivalry was all on him. He was the one reaching out, trying to match in some way the glamour and star-glitter of Stein. But it would be wrong to think of Hank as being merely a younger brother.

He was out-distanced, outshone by Stein. But he was also a young man of real talent and gifts of his own. I was caught in the middle in this clash of two human beings, both of whom I admired in different ways, over a number of years and a number of episodes.

They argued often, like stray cats on the fence. There was no doubt about Stein's ego, there was no question that he did ride roughshod over the kid brother or that Hank would try to impress Stein—and miss.

Once, on the boat, Hank took apart and put together an aneroid barometer. Later he asked Stein if that kind of barometer worked by mercury. Stein said, "Yeah, sure. I guess it works that way." So then Hank says, "Oh, no, you're wrong. It works with a spring basis, on a coil."

Stein looked at him across the deck, "For Christ's sake, what are you trying to do—be the big shot over a fucking barometer? What the Christ is the matter with you, Baron?"

There were times when Hank would miss the subtle underlying meaning, as in the episode with Pauline. Hank just hadn't caught the implications of what was going on there, while he nearly got blasted.

I could talk these things over with Hank because Hank had become really one of my best friends, probably the best friend I had in the world. I knew that the rivalry with his brother was real. Hank thought of himself as a writer and journalist. He felt he could challenge the great talent of Ernest Hemingway.

I had to agree it was a rough situation. Hell, he was up against one of the literary titans. This was a difficult situation for a younger brother striving to make it for himself.

Sometimes in our discussions, I'd say to him, "Listen, if it bothers you this much, why don't you simply change your name, Hank? Take another writing name."

His answer to that was, "Why should I change my name, Jake? I'm proud of it."

I said, "Well, if you don't, and you go into writing for a living, won't you be really riding on your brother's name, after all?"

Hank wasn't so sure. We talked often and long into the night about some other way out. I suggested our long cruise in the little yawl. We talked about getting a larger boat. The big dream was to circle the world, crossing to the Azores, Gibraltar, Suez, the Red Sea, India, Java. . . . It was such a magnificent goddam thing we were sitting there talking about and planning and dreaming.

But there were other ties Hank had to deal with: family ties, strong and persistent, the whole background out of which he came and to which he belonged. In none of that did I, or could I, have any real part.

Regardless of Hank's own needs or bitterness, there was no question that the Ernest Hemingway name had a magic that could open doors anywhere. It meant the top people, it meant official favors, it meant entry to any place you wanted to go—cocktail parties, the best clubs, government receptions, yacht races, the cream of the cream. That's how Stein's name worked in Havana and anywhere else in Cuba.

Part of the reason Hank Hemingway was so willing to go along on this world-circling sailboat ride was to prove something to himself, to Stein, and maybe the world—that he was something, a man with a real contribution to make. Sailing was one way he had it over his brother. But he could write, too; he could be a journalist and a damned good one.

This was the thing that was eating at him, and what we talked about.

Hank did, in fact, become a first-rate journalist, and wrote several books. One was a sort of family portrait he called *My Brother Ernest*. Another was a novel called *The Sound of the Trumpet*, a story about an American Army photography team that makes the D-day landing in Europe and goes on to Paris.

The story itself is not particularly unusual—a war love

story evolving in the midst of action. The style is reminiscent of Hank's older brother and follows Stein's frequently enunciated precept that a story should not be made up but has to come out of reality. Hank was in this kind of activity in World War II. And his brother was a famous correspondent.

Like his brother, Hank mingles reality and fiction skillfully so that identities are not so easily determined. Yet, in one or two bits of action, there are revealing overtones that could reflect the roles of the two men, Hank and his famous novelist/foreign-correspondent brother. The setting is Hemingway's familiar stamping ground, Paris, where the book's hero, Dan, and an associate arrive a few days after the city's liberation from the Nazis. One passage reads:

"They walked down the street to the Ritz. The lobby was deserted. From the shadows a well-dressed civilian stepped forward and introduced himself to the manager.

"'Gentlemen, the hotel is not yet open. What can I do for you?'

"'Is Randy Graham here?' Dan asked.

"The manager looked suspicious. 'But gentlemen, I have told you, the hotel is not yet open.'"

"'I understand about the hotel, but is my brother here?'

"'Ah, you are his brother. But, yes, of course.' He told them where to go, and apologized that the elevators were not in order. They walked up to Randy's suite. The door was open.

"'Ho there, Danno. How'd you make out? Ho, there, Todd.'

"'Well, but late. We didn't get in until yesterday. How did you manage to wangle a spot like this?' It was a suite, and the best.

"'Hell, we liberated the joint. Took a patrol through the basement and cleaned out some Krauts.'

"'Man, this is livin'. Do we celebrate?'

"Randy and the two other correspondents had found a smaller hotel nearer the Etoile that had a real food reserve and had swiftly become friends of the manager. He produced a turkey dinner that night while most restaurants, if open at all, were serving fried eggplant. A half dozen correspondents, the better looking females among them, were there. The biggest table didn't have enough places set. 'You sit over there, will you, Danno, with Billy, my fearless driver from the division? Billy, you know my kid brother. Here the waiter will get wine for you.'

"'Sure, Rando. It's a swell table.'

"Dan and Billy sat at the little side table and a waiter brought them champagne. There was real linen just like the big table, but it was like being ghosts and watching old friends at a banquet. The only candles were on the big table. They heard the laughter and watched people they both knew well, but in the dark and at the side they were neither seen nor heard. The food became dull and the wine had no effect.

"'Same way with you?' Billy said. 'Come on, let's walk around outside. After I drive them where they want to go we'll look up some people . . .'

"'It wasn't intentional,' Dan said. 'He didn't realize the big table couldn't hold everybody until he saw it.'

"'I know, I know.' Billy felt badly to have mentioned it but he had said what they both felt."

My own relationship with Stein was quite objective, because he knew that physically I could stand up to him and personally I didn't think of him as a rival. I admired him, respected his literary power, and accepted him as he was. This, again, was what I had discovered about Stein himself—he more or less accepted the world as it was. You and you and you were what you were and god damn it don't be bothering me beyond that point.

That was Stein. Take care of yourself; nobody around you is about to change your goddam diapers. There was no argument about this in his approach. It was a simple fact of life, ultimately overriding everything else.

There were times when I felt Stein really accepted me also as a brother. Not a blood kin of any kind; he had too much of the establishment base in his personal life to reject the traditional attitudes about kin. But I think he appreciated me for my own experiences, for my independence and refusal to knuckle down, even as he tried with his fists to cut me down to size.

It was actually a three-way relationship—Stein, Hank, and I. Hank and I were the two young bucks at that stage, out for adventure, thinking we knew everything, jabbering about sailing an 18-foot boat around the goddam world.

And the old bull was watching, the old boss bull who could go on a rampage any moment, was keeping an eye at least occasionally on what the hell we were getting into.

During our stay in Havana, and in Key West, Hank had developed a habit of writing letters back home to Oak Park, Illinois, full of exciting details about life in the subtropics. Hank had this quality of imagination and fantasy that he liked to give vent to in the way he told a story or remembered an incident.

It was a real talent, the way he could build details. Some

of the letters that got back to Illinois and Mother Hemingway were a little startling.

Hank had been raised carefully on the home front by his mother and sisters, and this journey of ours in the boat was the longest and farthest he had ever been from the close protection of the family home in Oak Park.

He must have been thinking that his mother and the girls up there would understand this was all in the way of humorous fantasying, but the ladies didn't take it that way.

He would write letters about adventures and things happening to him in the terror-filled Cuba that would send fears skyrocketing. At last Mother Hemingway wrote to her older son and asked, in effect, what the devil was going on down there. Hank's letters had been terrifying. One told of how a huge boa constrictor came down a tree Hank was sleeping under and Hank had to fight the creature off with his bare hands. . . .

One day on the *Pilar*, Stein boomed out to Hank, "Listen, Baron, will you, for Christ's sake, stop writing those wild letters to your mother? You want to scare her to death with a bunch of wild exaggerations? Sure, you're kidding. But for Christ's sake stop writing that kind of bullshit to your mother."

Stein was reading his mother's letter at that moment and he was really sore. He said, "Here's something about a fucking boa constrictor you supposedly fought with. Will you please stop this kind of crap before you give the woman a heart attack."

The truth was that Stein hated his mother with a deep hatred. He blamed her for the death of his own father and

he saw nothing good in her whatever. I also had a strange
relationship with my mother, but, god damn, I could see
her good side as well as all her kookiness.

Stein was at least taking his mother's side in this instance.

When I went to Oak Park some years afterward and met
Mrs. Hemingway for the first time, she said, "Oh, you're
Jake. You know, I'm so glad to meet you. Ernest wrote in
one of his letters that as long as his brother Leicester was
with you, I never had to worry."

And when Mrs. Hemingway—Stein and Hank called their
mother Gracie behind her back—told me that, I had a real
glow of pride.

Because Stein, by the time he wrote that letter, knew
about me and my background activities not only up North
but some of the doings I already had begun to move into
in Key West and Cuba. Sloppy Joe had filled him in on
some of the details.

And knowing, Stein still trusted me enough to write a
thing like that about my relationship with Hank.

Deserved or not, coming from Stein it was a real goddam
compliment.

## 12. A Young Man of Few Words

Hank and I moved around quite a lot; much of the tim
we were back in Key West, with Pauline and Stein and th
boys. I was leading a kind of double life in those days
partly with the Hemingways, partly off one of my ow
businesses with some of my former associates—includin,
Pico.

A lot of the time also I was out with the captains an
crews on the shrimp boats and turtle boats. They wer
really tough characters, but they knew the sea. This wa
where I learned to handle boats and ships.

Several times I came in on small boats carrying "cus
tomers"—alien Chinese. I knew as much about that filth
money-on-the-nose operation as Hemingway did when h
wrote his book about it, *To Have and Have Not*. Actually
I was a lot closer to it than Stein. Somebody once said h
used me as the character Harry in that book. But that wasn'
so.

In Key West Stein was not only a legend everybody knew about, but also a star tourist attraction. I can remember we used to go sunbathing with virtually nothing on in one secluded point outside the Hemingway home, and—my God —I'd be lying out there in the morning sun and I'd look up and see tourists gaping at us from the top of the nearby lighthouse.

There was a lot of gawking and gaping at the house and cars pulling up and stopping; sometimes people would try to get in. Stein was pretty rough on strangers intruding on him, in public bars or anywhere else. Usually he just turned away.

He had no time for that kind of crap. Still—the case of Arnold presented the exceptional outreach this man had, on occasion, even to someone he'd never seen before in his life. But it had to be damned special.

Stein had one basic rule I heard him reiterate many times: He would not talk about his writing as such, or about writing or writers. He sometimes discussed such things with his own friends, with Dos Passos, for example, or even Canby, but never with outsiders, sight-seers, celebrity hunters, or people like that.

And then this guy Arnold arrived, and all bets were off.

Arnold showed up one night at the house in Key West— it was about seven or eight o'clock—and knocked on the front door. We were all at dinner, but this Arnold was a good hard knocker and everybody could hear him way off. One of the help in the house opened the door and this fellow said he had to see Ernest Hemingway. He said it was very important.

Well, everybody had had a pretty good cocktail hour with rum drinks flowing free and Stein was feeling no pain and he stood up and decided he'd personally see what all the fucking noise was about.

And he got out there and he saw this lean young kid, about a year or so younger than Hank and me, standing in front of him. Stein gave this kid a quick once-over and said, "Yeah, what do you want?"

He said his name was Arnold. He said, "You're Ernest Hemingway. I want to study writing under you."

Stein said, "Well, I'll be god damned." He just stared at this kid and then asked, "How did you get here? Who sent you?"

"I'm a student of writing," Arnold stated calmly. "I bummed my way down here on a freight train."

"Jesus Christ," Stein said. "You mean, just like that you walk in?"

He had been studying writing in a Midwestern college, Arnold told Stein. He felt he could do better getting it straight from the horse's mouth. "I want to apprentice myself to you."

Arnold stood there in total, unruffled calm. I was pretty sure Stein had been rocked by this apprentice idea, but I also knew he needed a hand for the boat. Hank and I were too busy with our own affairs, and I had my outside activities. Stein needed somebody to wet-nurse the *Pilar* and polish the brass and keep the decks swabbed. And he was giving a hard once-over to this green kid who wanted to learn about writing first-hand from Ernest Hemingway.

It sounds strange that Stein would give this hoboing kid the time of day. He could have had a thousand applicants, ten thousand, the pick of the best writing talent out of the best colleges and universities. But this kid was there. Arnold had happened; he was on the scene.

Anyway, they came inside and talked, and several of us were standing around and Stein finally broke through all the hot air and said, "Do you know anything about boats, Arnold?"

"No, sir."

"Nothing at all?"

"No, sir. Nothing."

Arnold's greatest quality, I was to learn, was his ability to remain calm, whether he knew something or not, and no matter what great catastrophe might or might not be happening around him.

"Know anything about deep-sea fishing?"

"No, sir."

"Or fishing of any kind?"

"I never fished in my life."

Stein had a stubborn, bulldog tenacity. Writing was writing, but he needed a hand for the *Pilar* and here was a live one.

"Are you willing to work like hell on my boat and keep it cleaned and polished and in shipshape order so when we go out fishing we don't look like a pile of shit?"

"Oh, sure. Yes, sir. I can do that."

"You'd be willing to scrub, mop, hose down, do whatever you have to do?"

"Oh, I'll do anything. Anything."

Stein said, "Okay, Arnold. I'll give you a try. I'll give you an hour a day—well, maybe not a full hour, but once a day we'll talk. I'll look over what you do and we'll talk a little about it."

Arnold accepted this incredible thing in stride. But Stein added grimly: "But listen to me, Arnold. This is important. Except for that time we talk, don't you ask me one goddam word about writing any other time. Or mention it, even. Understand?"

I'd sort of ease in when they had their conversations; I was curious; it fascinated me. Much of what he said to Arnold in their discussions I seemed to know already, as though they were things I had absorbed about Stein's ideas over the months. The most important thing he kept drumming into Arnold was that you had to write out of the reality around you, not just out of your own mind. He kept telling Arnold that the occasional paragraphs he'd turn in sounded phoney. "Nobody'd believe you'd lived a word of that stuff."

One of the things that amazed me was the time and concern Stein took with this kid who just showed up like that. Then I got to thinking, hell, he accepted me, too. I just came here with Hank and he didn't have to buy me one way or the other. I was made part of the team. No questions asked. It seemed he just accepted me as he accepted everything else—on its own terms.

But this kid Arnold wasn't coming up with too much writing. He was working hard and overtime on the *Pilar;* he lived on the *Pilar,* actually, as well as keeping it Bristol bright. A number of times Stein lectured him about the lack of writing results. "You have to produce," he would say. "Don't be one of those people who talk a great story

84

they never write. Christ, you can't write anything that way. You can't talk; you have to produce."

Another thing I heard him stress a lot in talking with Arnold, as with a lot of other people, too, was honesty. Stein had a terrible thing about honesty. One thing I recall him telling Arnold was that you had to get the right word, the word that the particular character would use at a particular moment under the particular circumstances and situation. It was not just the *mot propre,* it was the *mot exact.*

He didn't say it that way. But that was what he was trying to get through to Arnold.

With Stein's usual penchant for giving everybody a nickname he began by calling Arnold "Maestro." This was because Arnold not only had ambitions of becoming a writer; he also had brought along his violin. But, after a few samples of his music and technique, everybody agreed that Arnold was not really symphony material. One evening, after hearing one number too many, Stein said to him, "Maestro, you can't play that violin for shit. We can't call you Maestro any more. We'll have to call you plain Mice."

Then he went on, "Besides, Mice—you're not getting anywhere in your writing. You can't just sit there talking about it, listening to me, or bringing in a couple of paragraphs. You've got to write a story, write whatever you want—but do it, finish it. Then show it to me."

Mice kept himself closeted up for a week in his cabin on the *Pilar.* Finally he showed up with a completed story.

Well, he'd written it and handed it in. And Stein read it. But Stein was pretty frank about it. "It's wordy as hell.

It's got too many goddam words and it doesn't say anything."

Mice told Stein, "But this is the way my professor at college up North taught me to write, with words and phrases like that. Flowing phrases."

Stein roared out at Mice, "What do you mean—your professor at college? If the son-of-a-bitch could write in the first place, he wouldn't be a professor in some college up North. He'd be writing himself. Are you going to listen to some goddam professor or are you going to listen to me?"

Mice hurriedly agreed that he wanted to learn from Stein and would listen to him. For some reason hard to put into focus, Stein really wanted to help this boy. Perhaps it was simply because Mice had shown up at the door that dinner hour, uninvited, asking for help.

Stein was really good to him and I admired him for this, because Mice got into difficulties even on the boat. He was smart and earnest but new at this business of fighting game fish. When you hook a big fish, for example, you have to stow all the lines, get everything set, get out still and movie cameras—one person would have the Graflex, another the Leica, a third the movie camera. It was all teamwork, taking the pictures, keeping everything out of the way of trouble during the fight. It was exciting—and demanding.

Mice's problem seemed to be that he was forever hooked into getting everything wrong. If his job was the movie camera, he'd put the thing on the tripod and the moment he started rolling film the goddam tripod would slip and he'd wind up with five minutes of mackerel sky. One time

Stein wanted a picture of himself in the fighting chair, but Mice was holding the camera backward and wound up with a picture of himself. Stein said, "Mice, you've got the goddamnedest picture of your belly I ever saw."

Stein would bawl the shit out of Mice on occasions, but he really didn't want to hurt him; he was only trying to draw whatever the kid had in him to the surface, to the fullest degree possible.

Mice kept writing things, once he got the flow started, and showing them to Stein, and apparently Stein must have caught some glimmer, because he said to Mice, "Mice, you've got to learn to throw out the stuff that's no good. You're keeping too much crap here. You've got to learn to keep the good and throw the bad stuff out. Throw the shit out."

Mice said, "But, Stein, how do I know which is good and which is bad?"

Stein looked at him with horror and astonishment. "You mean," he said, "you don't know the answer to that yourself?"

Mice said, "Well, gee, I'm not sure."

"Listen, Mice," Stein said, "if you're not sure about that, you will never be a writer. You can forget about it. Go back home to Minnesota and pick corn or rice or whatever you do up there."

"Oh, no," Mice said. "I want to be a writer. I have to be a writer."

My instinct told me Arnold's Key West adventure in literature was at an end or close to it.

Thinking back, it seems to me that I may have missed the

heart of what that Arnold episode really was about. It seems to me Stein, in this fortuitous adventure with this kid at the front door, may well have been consciously or subconsciously testing himself, his ability to deal with him, to teach him. Testing whether his own style of reality in writing, his lean reality, could be taught.

The fact was that he didn't teach Arnold very much. Certainly not in writing, and not much more in fishing or boating. Perhaps the truth is that he was not a teacher; we knew he loathed the pedantic and professorial as part of the phoney façade he always rejected.

Stein was a doer. If you wanted to learn his ways, you had to find answers in what he did—in the fish he caught, in the faces he occasionally bashed in, in the words he wrote.

Arnold was an experimental object for Stein, a test case that dropped in at the front door. And didn't work out.

Toward the closing days of Arnold's era, Stein was becoming more and more impatient, even cruel.

"You used to tell me you wanted to be a writer, Mice," Stein said one night after reading Mice's latest piece of writing. "Tell me, how much do you really want to be one?"

Arnold, after a long moment of thinking about this, said, "I'll tell you how much. If I really thought I couldn't be a writer, I'd shoot myself."

"You would?" Stein said. "Mice, I don't believe you have the guts to shoot yourself."

"Well, I don't know. I've never thought about that."

Stein said, "I'll tell you what, Mice. If you haven't the guts to shoot yourself, and you keep writing shit like this, don't worry about it. I'll shoot you myself."

I remember thinking that Stein didn't really mean it. He only shot wild game. Or was he about to make an exception?

Arnold, in any case, decided it was time to go home.

## 13. A Damned Good Time

*Everyone wanted to meet him, to see him, to know him. But he was not a public person. He talked to the world in his stories and books; for the rest, he respected his own right to privacy. He knew all types of people but selected only a handful as intimates. And they were drawn almost always from two groups—the very high and the very low.*

Stein was a hell of a lot of contradictions. I lived right with him and I'm a son-of-a-bitch if I could figure him out.

The house in Key West, for instance. An unpretentious, old-style Spanish house with floor-to-ceiling doors and windows, open beams, tile floors. It was Pauline's house, really. Pauline's money. Beautiful, full of that subtropic shadowy Spanish atmosphere, but not lavish or showy. It was a house that belonged in its setting, with its Spanish patterns and lore. It was part of the world of boats and breezes and docks and white-hot, subtropic sun.

They had a lawn on one side of the house that spread out quite a ways, and there were flowers and palmettos, and a flock of crazy peacocks that roamed the grounds. They lived loose and nested in the bushes, and they'd go around making the god-damnedest howl I ever heard. What they make isn't a call; it's a hysterical fit.

Pauline had built a swimming pool also—not pretentious, but a place where we could take a plunge without going down to a beach or the harbor. The carriage house, in the back, which went along with the grounds, was where Stein used to do his writing, in a little room on the second floor.

Often he would get up very early and write—sometimes as early as six or seven in the morning, and if the work was really going well, he would write till nine or ten in the morning. Hank and I slept in the coach house, but when Stein was working late or early, we'd spend the night on the boat.

It wasn't much of a work area Stein had for himself. Just a small upstairs room and a lot of clutter. Desk on one side, where he wrote, and a bunch of books and junk on the other, old pieces of bicycle, fishing tackle, baseball mitts, junk of that sort. The surface of the desk was always clear for him to work on, however. He'd write the first draft in pencil, and then he'd correct and revise that with the pen right over the first draft. I used to watch him cross out or write it with a pen. The third draft was on the typewriter. He typed himself, very fast, but two-finger style.

This was Stein's way. Today they would call it his life style: Work and toil at the typewriter. And a handful of cronies who were his only real friends. Cronies that didn't fit the big patterns, the big shots.

He was so big, so vital, everybody wanted to meet him. And he liked crowds, parties, going around to the bars, as long as there were no strangers pestering him. But his friends were people you never heard of.

One in Key West was a clerk in what was actually a hardware store and ship's chandler—Charles Thompson. His brother happened to be Sheriff Thompson, who at that time practically owned Key West and was a big landholder. And owned the ship's chandler's store where he let his brother clerk. Thompson also owned most of the turtle schooners, the ice plant, in that pre-electric refrigerator age, and a raft of local real estate.

The sheriff was an old-fashioned southern politician and businessman, clever enough to keep the good will of every group in the community. He was powerful and impressive.

Stein's crony and best friend wasn't the sheriff. It was the sheriff's brother, Charles, in the hardware store. Charles was big, physically big. A towering, soft-spoken, big man, very kind, very understanding. Charles had a speech impediment and couldn't pronounce his words correctly some of the time.

I knew Charles. We all did. We met him in the store or on the boat or at the house. I don't think I ever met a gentler man, always able to say the kind thing. I approved of Stein's friendship with Charles. I said to myself, "Stein is the kind of man an author should be. A man who cleaves to hardware clerks and busts a rich son-of-a-bitch on the chops when he tries to overtip and make the other guy look like a bum."

92

Another Stein crony was a fellow named Sullivan, who ran a boatyard in Key West where owners of small boats went for repairs and reoutfitting. This included most of those shrimp- and turtle-boat fishermen.

Sullivan wasn't just the boatyard owner for these men. He was their friend; when they got drunk, he got drunk; when help or food or aid was needed, Sullivan was there.

This was the second friend. Both were men of the common people—not the rich, not the famous. These men were not only Stein's friends; they were his suppliers: if the boat needed parts, he had to go to Charles Thompson; if it needed repairs, he had to go to Sullivan.

The third character in this collection was Sloppy Joe. Key West was where Sloppy Joe began—not in Havana or anywhere else. Joe—Josey, as Stein called him—was the original of the whole business. When he started, Key West had no tourists; it was a sleepy town at the curving edge of nowhere. But everybody in the Caribbean came there. Josey knew them all and they knew him—the bootleggers, the hired gunmen, smugglers, police, customs, the Coast Guard, the businessmen, the social set, the climbers, hoods, swindlers, killers.

I often wondered how the Christ Stein became so intimate with these people. Because of his hours of work, he lived like a recluse. And he wanted none of the adulation, none of the intrusions. He resented it and rejected it. Except for the inner circle, of which I had become a part, and for his few chosen local pals beyond that circle, he kept to himself. These three men became, in effect, not only cronies but his closest friends. A bartender, a ship's chandler's clerk, the boss of a boatyard.

Yet if you tried to approach him in a bar he'd turn his back on you that fast. Then, how did he meet the people he did accept? That was easy, once I thought about it. These were the people he needed in his daily life, in the real life of his daily world. Sullivan was the man who nurse-maided the *Pilar* and kept her in operation.

Charles, the clerk, was the guy from whom he bought his spare parts and needs for the boat. And Josey sold the booze. They were not only friends—they shared the intimacy of a 38-foot boat. They shared her problems, her replacement needs, her fittings, her inner soul.

Sloppy Joe was the moment of recreation, the center of talk and gossip, often the lifeblood of ideas and stories out of which Stein drew the spark and substance for a sizable portion of his writing.

We'd go over to Sloppy Joe's with Stein and his pals. Others would drop in, too—part of our group. We used to line up at the bar for drinks—only rarely did we sit at the tables. Big Skinner, a big, black Zulu, was the bartender. Big Skinner was also Joe's hatchet man if there was anything or anyone to take care of. If Josey didn't want somebody around, Big Skinner would make sure.

Big Skinner had a deep, rolling laughter—when he laughed. He also made all of Josey's smuggling runs with him. Skinner went out in a 30-foot powerboat that had two engines and was fast as hell. Josey got his start in booze in Key West, which was also a hot spot for smuggling of all kinds of stuff; almost anything you could think of that was illegal would come through the keys—Key West, most of all.

Coast Guard and customs people were there, too. Everybody knew everybody else. They'd go out and chase each other and nobody would ever get caught. Hell, sometimes you'd unload at the main Porter Dock, right in the heart of town.

The dock was five or six hundred feet long. Yachts and fishermen and some of the ferries to Havana used to tie up there. It was a colorful, busy spot—smelling with the odors of tropic fruits and cordage and cargo and tobacco and booze.

In the late afternoon Stein could relax with the people he could talk with or joke with or shout down.

Loosened by a drink or two, he forgot writing. Then it was all talk and booze and laughs and stories. Stein's mind seemed to move with the intensity of a trip hammer. Everything became amusing and delightful. He'd spin yarns about Paris or characters he knew or ran into. In these barroom moments I saw Stein at the warmest, perhaps the richest as a human being.

This was where Stein, with a few drinks under the belt, would spin a story and swing in a dozen other extraneous items before he reached the end, and the whole thing was an exciting embroidery of story and reality and people. He'd be talking about one thing and, Holy Christ, all of a sudden he was running down another byway. Or he'd see a beautiful dame come in and he'd give her the long once-over before he got back on the story.

This original Sloppy Joe's—the real original—was a beat-up old shack right across from the submarine base in Key West. The bar was a nothing and the floor was pure cement. Then the tourists began to come in after they rebuilt the bridges that had been swept out by a storm.

Stein liked the old small, shabby, and cheap joint Josey

had better than the new one he built. He used to tell a hell of a lot of stories in that old place.

One of those times he got half tanked up and started spinning a yarn out of his reporter days in Europe, when he was in Paris and had been there as a correspondent for the Hearst papers and was fairly well acquainted and knew the language pretty well.

The New York office cabled Paris that they were sending over one of their editors to give him a stint of foreign coverage. Stein didn't like this son-of-a-bitch, because he got the job only because his father was a friend of the publisher—one of those setups. Stein couldn't stand the guy. But word came that Stein was to break the editor in and take care of him while he was there.

Stein was livid that he had to squire all over Paris a guy he considered a pompous waster of time. He decided to give him a real fine welcome. For starters, he went down to the Left Bank and dug up some Paris apaches, gave them a few dollars, and rehearsed them in what they would have to do.

When the American editor arrived at the Gare du Nord, all these apaches were waiting to greet him. As the editor came through the gates Stein pointed him out, and all the apaches on signal began to cheer. There were forty or fifty of them at least, and the cheering could be heard all over the damn station. *"Vive l'Americain,* hurrah, hurrah for the American journalist. . . ."

The newly arrived editor swallowed the whole bit and puffed up like a pregnant pigeon. Then a couple of "reporters" Stein had hired came up to interview the editor and inquired how was the crossing and what did he think would happen in the French Government's latest crisis?

Stein shook the editor's hand, welcomed him in the name of the press, and said this extraordinary greeting could only mean that his fame was now international.

Later, as they walked up the streets of Paris, other people had been instructed by Stein to come up and say, "Oh, excuse me, aren't you the famous journalist from America?"

And when he admitted that he was indeed, they would shake his hand heartily and tell him, "Paris is honored."

Somewhat later, as they reached a large sidewalk cafe Stein frequented, a whole crowd of hirelings picked up the young editor and carried him, cheering and singing, through the Paris streets.

More than that, some of them followed him in his taxi to his hotel and insisted that he give them his autograph, which he willingly did. It was probably the most carefully prepared put-on in the history of modern Paris.

Nobody was feeling too sorry for the stuffed-shirt editor. But there was a note of Hemingway ruthlessness in it, too.

"Well, anyway," Stein insisted, "he went back to the States convinced he was the hero of Paris and the biggest success since the blowing up of the Maine."

Another of Stein's barroom stories concerned the inner operations of the Hearst syndicate, for whom at that time he was working. "The syndicate, at one stage, developed a bizarre concept for its overseas correspondents. It was either the cornucopia of plenty or the scorched-earth era."

One of the executives, he said, would tell a correspondent, "Now, you bastards aren't getting enough first-hand stories.

We have to beat out the competition and we don't care how you do it. If you have to bribe people, bribe 'em. Do whatever you have to do short of getting arrested, but get the story. We don't care if you have to buy the prime minister. That's all. You buy the son-of-a-bitch. We'll pay the bill."

"On the strength of that," Stein said, "we'd go out and work our ass off to get to top people, buy ourselves a couple of high officials and information that made a hell of a story. Then we'd send in the expense accounts. Understandably, floating around the bars of Paris, getting loaded with French big shots in the cabinet or Sureté, can run into tens of thousands of francs."

"Other Hearst correspondents," Stein said, "were going through the same shit in other capitals. The Hearst papers were doing a brisk business in newsbeats. But when the expense accounts began to pour into the comptroller's office, you could hear the anguished screams across the fucking ocean. The cornucopia stage was ended. Now it was the scorched earth. Top Hearst executives were furious. Nobody could spend a nickel, even if he had the King of England on his tab."

Stein had been holding a general in Paris on the string about some treaty-signing that was upcoming. The general was to give him all the information and bango! The closedown on spending put him out of business. No money to the general, no story for the wires. "But I'd already spent a wad of money getting the damn thing set up, buying drinks and broads."

As a result, Stein said he had been drawing heavily on his salary and expense allowance. But with the new, scorched-earth people in power, he began getting cables from the top man, and the cable would invariably begin: DEAR ERNEST OUR BOOKS SHOW YOU HEAVILY OVERDRAWN STOP PLEASE IMMEDIATELY CEASE ANY, ETC, ETC . . . It was always signed Frank.

Stein would cable a reply to the effect: DEAR FRANK TO GET STORIES MUST SPEND MONEY OUT POCKET STOP OTHERWISE COMPETITION WILL, ETC, ETC . . .

"The exchange of cablegrams went on for weeks," Stein said. "His always began with this cadaverous comment about what his books showed. I was tired of this son-of-a-bitch and his books. So I sat down and wrote one to terminate the whole matter."

In pure, basic Hemingway it read: DEAR FRANK: ADVISE UPSTICK BOOKS ASSWARDS REGARDS ERNEST.

Stein always had himself a damn good time. He loved to get drunk and talk. Once, on the *Pilar,* he was talking about the *lenguas largas*—the long tongues—a name some gave the Cubans because they are great on the gab. It's talk, talk, on the street, in the restaurants, at bars.

Stein said, "On the other hand, in Mexico, the men don't talk much. Hardly at all. But they have big balls. That's what they say.

"To Mexicans, the term big balls means strength. This is also the term in Spanish. When they say big balls, it means a man really has it."

Stein was sitting on the boat fishing when he was telling us about this. And he said, "You know what they ought to do? They ought to send a shipload of Cuban long tongues

99

from Cuba over to Mexico and swap them for a shipload of Mexican balls. Then the Cubans would stop talking and screw."

Stein and I got on great at these parties. And, like him, I was having a damned good time. I could match him drink for drink any night, and Stein approved of that. You had to take your drinks like a man or not at all. With Stein, you had to take things seriously—even having a ball or getting laid.

It was odd about Stein and me. It was as if I was drawn to him by forces of our two natures, as if some part of me was him, as if he needed and used me—a big, overcocky kid at that time—in order to understand something about his own strength and weakness.

He was a 38-foot powerhouse roaring to glory down the channel. I was a tramp in the night. I would go by another way. Yet our lives touched.

## 14.  Scars

We were sitting side by side in the fishing chairs on the *Pilar*, Stein and I. He was in one of those moods in which he didn't talk. He'd go like that sometimes for hours without saying anything. Literally sometimes not a word.

I didn't understand that part of him at first; I thought he was just being plain moody. Brooding. But it wasn't that. Stein was thinking, pondering something, working something out, some hitch, some problem in the shaping in his mind. He was letting the character, and the words that character had to say, take shape. That's what I came to realize.

When he wasn't in one of those pondering spells, Stein was one of the most engaging talkers I ever heard. His humor was always there. But in this other state of mind he was another person. He was a human being apart.

I was pretty mature for my age, but this was one phase of him I had not fully grasped. I knew it was something

101

special that he let me sit there beside him without feeling that I was an intruder or a disturbing influence. I liked being on the *Pilar* anyway; I had my own thoughts to think—thoughts and possibilities I did not share with Hemingway.

So we sat there in this wordless communion, side by side in the fishing chairs, gazing out at the water, the boats, the shoreline and sky.

Half an hour went by. Then it was a whole hour. An hour and a half. Two hours. Not one word spoken by either of us in all that time.

What began for me as something casual became after two hours a terrible burden of silence. A growing tension that had to be broken. I thought to myself, "Christ, I've got to break this thing up. It's too overwhelming."

That silence on the afterdeck of the *Pilar* was explosive. Stein was sitting there beside me, dressed only in his shorts. I'd never noticed before how much of his body was scarred. It was really a mass of scars, especially on his legs. These scars, I'd been told, were the result of being seriously wounded in World War I when an enemy shell splattered shrapnel all over him. I have heard one or two reports that Stein was nicked in the testicles but not seriously enough to cause any permanent damage. There were certainly scores of fragments in his lower limbs. And the early fear that some of these might have impaired his virility—which it didn't—was clearly Stein's springboard for *The Sun Also Rises*.

He was a brooder about some of those things. But he let it out in his writing. Maybe it was therapy for his subconscious fears that what happened to his hero, Jake, in

*The Sun Also Rises, could* have happened actually to him. As in one passage in the book, when Jake and his girlfriend Brett are in a taxi in Paris:

" 'She had been looking into my eyes all the time. Her eyes had different depths, sometimes they seemed perfectly flat. Now you could see all the way into them.

" 'When I think of the hell I've put chaps through. I'm paying for it all now.'

" 'Don't talk like a fool,' I said. 'Besides, what happened to me is supposed to be funny. I never think about it.'

" 'Oh, no. I'll say you don't.'

" 'Well, let's shut up about it.'

" 'I laughed about it too, myself, once.' She wasn't looking at me. 'A friend of my brother's came home that way from Mons. It seemed like a hell of a joke. Chaps never know anything, do they?'

" 'No,' I said. 'Nobody ever knows anything.' "

Looking at those scars as we sat there, I decided that would be as good a way as any to break the wordlessness that had been going on for two hours. So I said, "Jesus, I never realized, Stein. You've got a hell of a lot of scars."

It was a stupid thing to say. Absolutely stupid. But this was in the early period, when I first went down there. I thought I was somehow starting a conversation, breaking into this almost paralytic silence.

I knew Stein wasn't vain enough to worry about his beauty. But he just about bit my head off, more or less. He said, "Well, the scars are there and there's nothing I can do about it, is there?" Then he turned and looked at me. "You want to do something about it?"

103

Stein could really be nasty when he wanted.

I just shut up. And he didn't say anything else eithe we went right back into the silence. This time, however, was relatively brief—perhaps ten or fifteen minutes. Knov ing Stein, I was sure by that time he would realize he real had been unreasonable in his outthrust at me. I believe that was what was happening.

In any case, he turned abruptly to me and said, "Jak Hank tells me you come from up around our country?

I said, "Yeah. My home's in Iowa. About two hundre miles west of you." Then he wanted to know what town was and I said, "Oh, you wouldn't know it. It's a very sma town—Mount Vernon."

Stein said, "Mount Vernon, Iowa? Sure I know it. Don they have a little college there?"

I was really startled. I said, "How would you know abou Cornell College?"

And Stein said, "Well, god damn it, I ought to kno it. Pauline's family just gave them a dormitory."

"Jesus," I said, "that costs real dough."

"Costs like all hell," he said. "But that's not all. Re member that friend of hers I conked on the chin when th silly bastard tried to double my ten-dollar tip? He's goin to give them another new dormitory—double the size the Pfeiffers'."

## 15.  Death-Time Story

Two days after Pauline arrived from Key West to break up
Stein's fandango with the lady on the *Pilar* in Havana Harbor, Hank and I decided the time had come to blow town.

The atmosphere had changed. All the joking and laughter, the big time, the big talk, the excitement, were suddenly gone. Pauline sat on the *Pilar* like a freight-yard bull
with a shotgun; everything took on a morgue-like atmosphere. The damper was really on. It was time for Hank and
me to pull out.

We set out in the yawl, with its mainsail and mizzen,
trying to beat our way along the northern Cuban coast,
heading east. This boat we were in, this yawl, was really
just nothing. Stein still insisted she wasn't safe enough to
take out beyond the harbor breakwater.

The trade winds in that part of the world are nothing to
fool around with either. The trades go through their patterns like a prearranged dance. At night they seem to rise

high in the sky, and then it is calm over the land. About ten in the morning they spring up and start to blow, and by three o'clock in the afternoon they howl like a bastard. Then the heat of the day has built up and a cloud forms over the land gathering moisture; a big cumulo-nimbus builds up, and along about four o'clock in the afternoon squalls set in with almost hurricane force. They can smash you to shreds if you don't take in sail quick. It's a real goddam routine.

You do get a warning; you see a big black line, the storm line, near the horizon, growing bigger and coming straight at you. And you get your ass off the deck and start reefing in and getting ready for it. Then it hits. Comes down rain like a bitch for about an hour and then slacks up.

That's the sea around Cuba. There is an inland waterway that runs for miles along the northern coast. We went in there and dug our way along routes almost impossible to follow. They had no real markers, nothing but stakes to mark the channels. Some of the stakes were nothing but a small twig you could hardly see, sticking six inches out of the water. We got onto it after a while, after going aground over and over.

We kept heading east, with Haiti as first destination beyond Cuba. After that it was to be Puerto Rico, the Windward Islands, South America. If we made it.

One important thing on the yawl was that Hank Hemingway and I came to understand each other. Anyway, I came to understand him more, because he poured out a great deal about himself and his family that made his own role in life and his own personality clearer to me. I didn't

talk nearly so much about myself to Hank, or to anyone.
I had learned the importance of not talking. In the rail-
yard jungles, on the freights, in the other activities I got
involved in, you learned to listen.

We were young, we were learning the world, but you
can't bum around half of the ocean up and down the coasts,
day and night, in the same small boat, and not get to
understand a guy and his problems.

I was something else. I kept having the feeling that I had
a hell of a lot to see and do and not much time to do anything. I really felt I had to do it alone. I didn't want en-
cumbrances. God, no. I would go all by myself; I was on
my own. No close ties, no people, no girl, no wife. Nothing
to bind me permanently to anything.

I traveled alone and traveled swiftly. I had to move like
the wind. Anything that came up that sounded interesting
or profitable I'd listen to. Just about anything except dope
or murder.

We beat our way together some four hundred miles along
the northern coast. Much of it followed those inland channels, dodging in and out of the reefs. A small boat like ours
is no good in the really rough weather on open seas; about
that, Stein had been right as hell. Several times we had to
spend days—even a couple of weeks—waiting behind one
of the reefs, living as best we could on canned supplies,
fresh fish we caught, coconuts and bananas, whatever we
could find along the beaches.

At night we would sit and talk, as young people do. Two
of us in that boat with darkness, night, stars, and quiet.
Nothing but the sound of the water against the beach.

107

One of those nights, Hank got to talking about his father and his mother and about his father's death.

It was a large family, Hank explained. The Hemingways had five children: Hank and Stein and three daughters. Their mother—Gracie, as they called her behind her back—had been a beautiful girl from Oak Park. She was a big woman and had studied to be an opera singer. Ernest looked like her, especially the face and the tall figure, Hank said. When I first saw her, some years afterward, she still wore long, old-fashioned dresses.

Hank seemed almost to forget I was there on the boat at all. It was as if he were telling me because he himself wanted to hear it again, as if it really tormented him.

When Grace first met her husband, Dr. Clarence Hemingway, he was a young surgeon, very talented, full of high standards. He was also a handsome and highly sexed guy. He cared about people. And was gone on this tall, beautiful dame he was to marry.

The practice that developed in later years of young couples shacking up together prior to actual marriage was not acceptable in those days, particularly not with people like the Hemingways. The young surgeon looked for marriage with a woman whose beauty would be matched by the warmth of her response. In those late-Victorian times you didn't ride the horse before you bought it.

Hank told me that after Clarence and Gracie were married, he discovered she was virtually frigid—she could have children, but she could not meet his father's need for a real love, a real relationship or response. In her eyes, sex was still the symbol of man's evil and woman's burden.

But his father, Hank said, had strong principles: he

108

wasn't about to commit adultery; he wouldn't have dreamed of taking a mistress or going out to the Indian reservation and getting a girl for a few bucks, which a lot of other men did. Whatever he did or didn't do, however he managed, the fact was that his own loneliness for real love must have been plain, unadulterated hell.

He felt frustrated, trapped, and he bore it as long as he could. There must have been other frustrations, but the most important was clearly the lack of love on the part of the one person from whom he needed it most.

Finally, after years of this, he went up to his room, put a pistol in his mouth, and pulled the trigger and killed himself.

Stein had been close to his father, and subconsciously blamed his mother for this terrible thing. And he hated her; he really hated Gracie. Oh, God, how he hated her.

Stein knew that if you're highly physical, you have to do something. His father wasn't a monk, wasn't cut out to be a monk. Nor was he merely a family stud. And he couldn't cheat, because of this streak of honor in him. Stein himself reflected that streak not in sex but in other ways: in his writing, in his dedication to integrity, in his talks with me about the importance of law.

Stein used elements involving some of the incidents of his father's suicide later, in a story entitled "Fathers and Sons."

"I'm twenty years younger than Stein," Hank said. "I was sixteen years old. But this was something I can't forget—ever. I remember it almost like something that happened

109

today—yesterday. I see it in front of me now, this moment. And it was months—years—ago."

Around us were the buzzing sounds of insects and the night and the waves beating on the beaches beyond the barrier reefs.

He was looking off into the darkness and I could almost feel that he was actually seeing this thing in front of him. He told me he heard the shot and rushed into the room to find his father dead and the room splattered with his father's brains and blood.

"That scene," Hank said, "will be with me as long as I live."

## 16. Salvage

The other side of my life, the Hemingways did not know about or understand. I neither condone nor excuse any of those things I became involved in. I was what I was. Young, uncivilized, determined to make a life of my own. Short or long. But mine.

Stein, who was guarded in his approach to me about these things, once said to me, "Jake, what the hell are you getting into?"

"Jesus," I said. "You work hard to make money doing it your way, writing. I work hard my way."

He gave me a long look, measuring me as if I were some fucking dead fish hanging on a hook.

We all have our codes. Different codes, which each of us lives by. Codes for geniuses and bums, killers and thieves and scoundrels.

As I saw it, Stein was a pistol-hot good reporter. And he was much more, because he had imagination, too. He took

111

life and reality around him, and then he remade it, reshaped it, in depth that made a character naked and defenseless—in one single sentence.

He was wild, erratic, and a potent drinker. He was also conservative. He liked to be nonconformist within the bounds of what was in some ways ritualistic acceptance of the establishment. And I wasn't establishment; I had sworn never to get civilized.

He was worried, however, about my occasional disappearances from the scene for a day or two or a week, in Key West or Cuba. In Key West he had a real suspicion about the Chinamen—and the fear that I was in with the smugglers.

Stein insisted the novelist had to find basic novelistic reality out of his own reality and experience. If he had drawn me for some character in *To Have and Have Not*, his novel that centered around smuggling Chinese into Florida, he would have been accurately following his own dictum. I was a part of it. So was Sloppy Joe—whom Stein did use in the book.

Reading the book, I was surprised at so much that Stein knew and pictured in that story. Much of it had come through his friend Josey; he knew all these people and characters and all the corruptions of Key West and environs. There was one hell of a lot of corruption.

I actually made only two trips on these boats with their miserable cargo moving into the deserted palm-tree harbors in the keys, getting the "passengers" ashore (sometimes through heavy surf) at a fee of a thousand each—a lot of money in those days—and sending them North via the half-fare Franklin buses on US 1.

Some of what Stein wrote in the book was not totally accurate, based on my own experiences, but it doesn't matter. The errors concerned transient details. The heart of it was truth. I got to know the routine well, including the hoods such as Pico who ran it; it was a god-damned business, a god-damned deadly business.

Unfortunately—and not with any direct intent to do so—I was using one of the world's greatest authors as a front for the underworld, as a cover for my own activities as a smuggler.

This is the truth. It is a truth I regret.

And yet Stein knew. All the time, he also had the truth. Sloppy Joe kept him informed. But Stein said nothing directly to me or to anyone else.

I was still virtually a member of the Hemingway family; I was Hank Hemingway's closest friend. On our first trip down the northern coast of Cuba we were in the 18-foot yawl. Later, Hank purchased a sloop, the *Golden Eagle,* a 32-footer, a beautiful boat. I put in some money; now that I had a source of income, I could occasionally pay my own way for things. We were still talking of the big cruise south to Brazil and around the Horn; we could beat our way alone, the two of us, around the world.

We got as far as Nuevitas, a city about four hundred miles east of Havana, on the north coast. An old city and a sleepy one, with all the warm smell and aromas of the tropics—a kind of Cuban-Spanish pink stucco backwash. Hank and I spent a lot of time in that community, but

we went in different ways. Hank moved in his own circles
the American consul and his headquarters were a center
of social life in Nuevitas. Hank enjoyed that part, and he
spent some of the time at the Spanish Club—ladies in
flowing dresses and gentlemen in white linens. Hank liked
to talk also with freighter captains who dropped into the
consulate.

We were still close friends, but I wanted no part of the
social hogwash. Hank could have it, but mostly he had to
count me out. I did go to some of the formal parties and
that crap. Wives in their big-brimmed hats making plays
for the men—usually somebody else's husband. High-society sex under the palms.

I was already moving in other areas. I never mentioned
my new interests to Hank when we were together on the
sloop, anchored out on Bahía de Nuevitas. He didn't ask
questions; I didn't volunteer answers.

Most of the time I was down along the Nuevitas waterfront. I was hanging around in the dives and homes and
hovels of fishermen, of the Cuban poor. I was with the
Cuban revolutionaries of that day.

They were a world apart, a world Stein himself never
really knew, not as I did. I made these people my buddies;
I went out with them on their fishing boats and their
shrimp boats and their dinghies, going for bottom fish and
setting pots for crayfish. I went with the sailors and fishermen and the charcoal burners, the working men. Some of
these were the so-called Abecedarians, as they were known,
from the initials, ABC, of their political party that planned
to take over the government from the current dictator and
turn it into a free country.

114

I was to help these people, for a price, with other things. With guns and ammunition and dynamite.

All this was long ago, in the early era of Batista, a repressive era in which various political parties and groups were still struggling for the right to speak out and Batista was carrying on a strong effort to repress all opposition.

They talked with me about these things in their homes and boats and drinking holes. One goddam restaurant was built on piles right over the blue-green water. You sat at bare wooden tables—they had candles and kerosene lamps —and we would get loaded and talk and sing and argue. You could spit right into the sea through the slats on the floor. It was a real art. It took practice.

These people I was with trusted me. I was the American kid, but they would tell me their plans for fighting Batista; they would discuss their need for guns and ammunition. I had already been involved bringing Chinese into the keys. I had contacts with other sources. We talked about what I could do for them as I sat there in the waterfront bar getting loaded on rum, talking with them about their work and their poverty and their families and the dictator who had taken over their freedom.

We were in two different worlds, Hank and I, at that stage. He was up there reading the glossy magazines and mingling with the banana-boat captains that dropped in to make a noise. That was Hank's bag. Mine was down here at the other end of the pole.

Despite these things, Hank and I shared a number of adventures on the first sloop and later on the *Golden Eagle*. One of those adventures on the *Eagle* mixed up the two worlds—the subtropic socialites and visitors and the fishing-boat people and the *carboneros* in their carts.

It began off the coast near Bahía de Nuevitas—a big bay lined with palms, beaches, jungle, and fishing villages. We were cruising off the coast when we came upon some fishermen apparently trying to bring in an abandoned vessel—a large, white sloop.

Her name was the *Seal* and she was forty feet long. She had gone aground off Nuevitas just inside the outer reef and had holed her bottom. Some of the fishermen had spotted her and decided to bring her in. As an abandoned derelict on the open water, she could be claimed by them as salvage.

The *Seal* was owned by a writer who was down there on a honeymoon with his bride. Hank got the reports later at the U. S. Consulate: the couple had been cruising along the coast, hit the reef, and went straight over it into the calm shallows beyond.

All this occurred on a calm, clear, moonlit night, when just that kind of thing does happen, because the night is beautiful and full of shadows and the sea is calm and no water is breaking over the reef, so there's no sound to warn you, no white lines of breaking water.

The shipwrecked bride and groom got safely ashore, looked at the damage, and decided that repairing the sloop was simply impossible—at least for a young couple on their honeymoon. They abandoned it as a total loss.

So there it was—the sloop and the fishermen trying to bring it in.

Hank and I agreed to join the fishermen trying to get the boat back to where she could be repaired. It was no simple task. We agreed to use the *Golden Eagle* in this operation—but we had no motor and had to do everything by wind and sail.

This required maneuvering with our lines. We took our throat halyards and brought them to the *Seal*'s masthead —she was on her side in the water like a huge, dead bird. We righted her and then brought her mast down and across our deck, because the hole was in the bottom and by pulling the mast down and making her fast to our sloop we had the hole in the bottom exposed and could set to work putting on a jury-rigged canvas cover.

When it was low tide, we put the canvas over the hole and nailed it firmly to the hull. That was the first step. Second was to put tin over the canvas and nail that to the hull. We then had to deal with the water inside her; we righted her and began pumping her out.

All this was done primarily by the fishermen themselves with our aid and occasional suggestions. And our sloop. Once we got the water out of the hull, we and the fishermen together towed her, with her high mast rising against the skies, back to the Nuevitas harbor.

We were towing, of necessity, by sail. It was tricky and difficult, handling the *Seal* under those conditions. She slewed and yawed like a bitch on a bicycle all the way back.

Hank and I and the fishermen got the battered honeymoon sloop across the Bahía de Nuevitas and into the fishermen's wharf, where they intended to reoutfit her and use her as the new queen of their fishing fleet.

I hadn't realized that Hank was already setting in motion, in the consulate's office and back in the States by mail, a plan to claim salvage rights.

I told Hank he was wrong. He didn't understand the fishermen as I did. We had helped. Our boat had provided a means by which they could bring her in. But they had done most of the work. It was their prize, not ours.

I never said or believed Hank didn't have his faults. But he always had plenty of real guts. Even to admit when he was wrong.

He was sitting there in the cockpit of the *Golden Eagle;* we were anchored out in the bay. And he turns and says, "Jake, damn it, you're right. I kept thinking we could get the papers, we *could* technically claim salvage. They couldn't have done it without the *Eagle*. But I wasn't thinking from the other side, their side. Without them, nobody would have had her. She'd have broken up."

I was glad to hear him say that. And the fishermen who had heard reports they might not get title were elated.

We were on the *Golden Eagle* a couple of weeks later when we saw the *Seal* coming by in the late afternoon, sails full with the wind and the fishermen yelling and waving at us. That was a beautiful sight.

## 17. A Cuban Cul-de-Sac

*I was involved in a dangerous game with dangerous men. I was a pirate—a smuggler of human and other contraband. I was no longer broke. I even had money enough to buy my own schooner, a pretty big one with myself as skipper and a crew of characters straight out of the dregs.*

*It was a life and a pattern of operations totally apart from my associations with the Hemingways. Hank knew nothing about any of it.*

*I was in one of those port cities not too far from Havana. Hank and I visited there once in the Eagle. And I later returned there, alone, on my own business. Hank was back on the American mainland. . . .*

I was bringing a cargo of guns and bullets into that port—for delivery, as usual, to the anti-Batista underground.

One of the top people in the port was an American State

Department official. I had met him earlier at a couple of yacht club parties we attended in Havana.

It was a matter of business, personal business, as far as he was concerned. But important. Almost a matter of life or death.

I was cautious as all hell, in this business I was in. I had the stuff stowed well below decks in the foreward hatch, well hidden by other, harmless stuff on top. There are a lot of islands and reefs all along that northern coast, and I played a real game of hide and seek in and out of the island. I had plenty of supplies; I watched every step of the way. I would hide a cargo of guns on an offshore island for a week or two while I "cased" the *bahía* and the port. I had no desire to face a Batista execution squad.

I'm sitting on the schooner waiting for the contact to come out and set up the rendezvous. No lights on and I'm shooting the breeze and drinking and fucking—I've got a woman on board.

One of the sailors says, "Hey, there's a *gringo* coming out here in a rowboat."

"*Gringo?* There aren't any *gringos* around here," I tell him. "I'm the only *gringo*."

He says, "Yeah, I know. But there's one coming now. I can hear the oars and I spotted him. He's white."

It was just about dusk, and with the darkness closing in you couldn't see. If some guy were coming to get me, he'd come later, when I was asleep. I wasn't too worried. And the boat comes up alongside and, holy Christ, it's this State Department character I'd met earlier in Havana.

He said he wanted to talk with me, and I said, "Why, sure, come aboard, friend."

120

I thought maybe he'd gotten word of what I was doing. We went down to the cabin aft, where nobody could hear us, and he said, "I'm in trouble."

I said, *"You're* in trouble?"

I was greatly relieved. "You remember, in Havana," he said. "I told you I gambled. You remember?"

I said, "Yeah, now it comes back to me. You used to have regular poker parties out here, you said. Big ones."

I also remembered he said it was his one consuming problem. He didn't step out with women and he didn't drink. But he was a compulsive gambler. And he said, obviously very distraught about this, "I've got myself in a spot. I dipped into the petty cash for a thousand dollars."

His voice actually almost broke as he told me this. "The United States Government is very careful of how its civil servants spend U.S. funds. I've been on a losing streak. I had to find cash to cover my losses. Now I've learned this afternoon that one of our top executives is making an official inspection here tomorrow, about noon.

"I figured it out," he went on. "He'll find the discrepancy almost at once. It's that obvious. In the office there's just so many American dollars on hand. And a thousand of them will be missing. I can't let it happen. My whole career is at stake. Can you understand? I've got to find a thousand American dollars tonight. Not Cuban dollars. They've got to be American."

I didn't say anything for a moment. Only waited. After a minute he added, "I can't borrow it from any Cubans; they'd know what I'm doing or did. Anyway, they couldn't get American dollars."

Another silence. I wasn't about to commit myself. And

121

then he said: "You're the only one who's got them that I can turn to."

Of course, he gave no indication that he knew what I was doing or what kind of cargo I had carried into that port. I said to him, "What makes you think I've got dollars at all? I'm just a poor trader."

He said, "Oh, I know you've got it."

Well, that struck me, the way he said it. I said, "How come you're so sure?"

"Because in the business you're in, brother, you've got to have at least a thousand dollars in your pocket."

And, of course, it was true. With a cargo of guns and ammo sitting under me, waiting for delivery to the rebels, I had to have a wad of cash big enough to deal if I had to. I was no longer broke; I no longer had to live off anybody. This State Department man across from me was right. I had the money; I had to have it on hand. It could be anything, any emergency.

All he said was, "I'll pay you back the whole thing in two weeks."

I gave him the thousand. I could afford it, all right. Living on the boat alone was cheap. A couple of my associates would join me in a day or two. I was never hurried by anything. You co-ordinate with people; you move in and out easily, in and out of coves; you plan the point, the drop, where you leave material to be picked up later. There were all kinds of ways.

You always had to worry about two things; whom you were suspicious of and who was suspicious of you. Sometimes I'd unload our stuff out in the keys and come in

122

empty. Just in case somebody came aboard for a look, some police boat or customs people. Finding a spot in the keys to leave stuff was no problem. God, I knew places you wouldn't believe.

The hurricanes shaped and reshaped those channels and keys, cut new channels through them, plowed right through them with a slash seven feet deep. You could sail right into those places, right up to the shore, the way the hurricanes cut channels through.

I gave the American the thousand he needed to save his skin and his diplomatic career. I figured, well, he owed me a favor. One day I might have to collect.

The official kept his word, too. He showed up two weeks later with the thousand, rowing out and rowing back, just as he had the first time.

Very shortly after the episode with the official and the thousand dollars, I was again out on the schooner, alone this time, when I heard the sound of oars coming toward the boat.

It was an unusual, clinking sound that indicated to me that it wasn't any of my friends, because they used rowlocks made of rope, not metal, and this sounded like the metal rowlocks that were used mostly by the police.

The clinking sound was getting closer and I was becoming more and more frightened. Somehow all my background seemed to know the sound or smell of police. I knew it had to be cops. Wearing only a pair of shorts, and a knife, I dived over the side as the boat grew closer. Then I swam under water two hundred feet, heading directly away from the boat.

123

Powerful spotlights began sweeping the whole area around the boat and I could hear the rat-tat-tat of machine-gun bullets peppering the water.

The police were sweeping around with the guns, trying to find me with those bullets. I kept below the surface as long as possible, swimming under water as far as I could and coming up out of range of the boats and the light. They kept circling around the boat, apparently believing I would stay close to the boat and must be treading water in the dark.

Instead, I swam toward shore—heading for the mangrove swamp, sticky, muddy, full of disease, insects, snakes, a vicious, terrible place, unfit for any form of human life. It was almost two miles off. This was where I could hide. They would not dream I would pick this fever-infested hell spot. Or if I did, that I would ever come out alive.

I didn't go into that swamp by chance. That official I'd loaned the thousand to owed me something, and he was about to have a chance to pay me back, provided I lived that long. My plan was to work my way—under cover of night—through the swamp to the city, close to the official residence where he lived.

For two weeks I lived in those swamps, crawling my way at night, in the darkness, toward the city. I lived on land crabs and mussels growing on the mangrove roots—anything edible. I drank the goddam deadly swamp water—a few drops—just enough to keep from going out of my mind from thirst. I was practically naked, I had a thick beard, I'd lost pounds, I was half alive, half dead.

I stayed in that wet hell for two weeks, not knowing how long I could last or when I'd be grabbed by the cops. Then I inched my way to the town with its narrow sidewalks and stucco houses lining the streets. After making it there, about 2 A.M., I got to the street where the official lived, and weak as I was, I climbed hand over hand up the outer wall of one of the houses, hanging onto vines, notches, rainspouts, windowsills, whatever I could grab onto, all the way up to the roof.

Everything was pitch black. But I edged my way softly, walking most of the time on my toes, across the rooftops to the house where this man lived. I was still wearing only the ragged pair of swimming trunks and my knife. I had nothing else. I looked like the wrath of God.

Part of the top floor of the quarters where the American lived was a roof garden; the door leading from the roof into the house itself was unlocked. All the doors were unlocked. Nobody used that part of the house much, I had learned, so I hid up there for three more days, watching and waiting for a chance to catch him alone.

In his bedroom, on the floor below, he took a siesta from eleven to two each day while everybody else was out to lunch. I would sneak part-way down, trying to catch him there alone. It was three days before I got the chance. He was sleeping in his hammock under a mosquito net. I drifted into the room quietly, and sat down in a corner so I wouldn't startle him when he opened his eyes.

I sat there like a ghost. Then—softly—I called out his name. He opened his eyes, looked startled as hell, and then he saw me. He was bewildered, of course. I told him the whole story. And I said, "Look, all I want you to do is to hide me upstairs in the attic where nobody goes, lock me in there and get me food and water and for Christ's sake don't tell a living soul I'm here."

I told him then that I'd been dealing with the charcoal burners who were part of the revolutionaries and I wanted him to get to one of these charcoal men and send him up to me. So he ordered a fresh supply of charcoal, and when the guy arrived sent him up to me. The charcoal burner knew about my business and promised to get me out of there safely. He said, "They've been wondering what happened to you. They know the police got your schooner. They thought you'd been arrested or maybe shot and thrown to the sharks."

I said, "Nothing like that. I just want to get out safely."

We worked out a plan that they'd deliver some bad charcoal in the next day or two, the cook would complain, and they'd have to come and collect the stuff because it would be too hard and wouldn't burn well. But when they took away the bad stuff in the sacks, one of the sacks would be carrying not charcoal but one pretty hefty human being.

The State Department official was extraordinarily pleased to see me carried out of there in that cul-de-sac exit. Within a few days I was back in Havana and on up to Key West. But I had lost my schooner. The Cuban police took that for their prize.

I had saved the American from scandal and ruin. And he had saved me from arrest, possibly a firing squad. We were both guilty of our private crimes. Which was why each of us was in a position to help the other.

I thought the whole thing was odd and ironic. It had the elements of a Hemingway yarn, come to think of it. And I was the chief character. The chief stupid son-of-a-bitch.

## 18. To Have . . . and to Lose

*Stein knew.*

*I couldn't say how much, but enough.*

*The word had gotten back to Josey. The people I'd been dealing with in Havana were part of the crowd. It was Pico, for one. And a guy called Honest John, a first-class entrepreneur of crime. I first ran into Honest John in the Uncle Sam Bar, in Havana. He looked, acted, and talked like a character out of some Latin-flavored gangster movie. He was small, thin, wore highly polished shoes and spats, a white goatee, and a wide-brimmed Spanish fedora hat. Everything about Honest John was punctilious—to the last string of his slicked-down hair.*

*I got a hint of how it was when Honest John, who worked with me and Pico in the gunrunning business, casually told me once, when I was heading from Havana up to Florida with a boatload of Chinese, "When you get to Key West don't forget to give Josey my regards."*

Stein never said anything outright, direct. It was always by indirection. He'd let it come out in a few slanting things that I couldn't miss.

The night after that knife episode, for instance. We sat out there on the *Pilar* talking till almost everybody, excluding Carlos, was gone.

Stein had a pretty big load on that night. When Stein had too much, it didn't really show as it did with other people. It only seemed to magnify his mood, whatever that mood was. I don't remember Stein ever getting staggering drunk. You could tell he'd been drinking only because he'd become exuberant, boisterous.

He was half drunk, I'd say. It was almost worth losing the knife and taking the clout on the head he gave me when he pulled me back from diving into the harbor. Because he got very confidential with me after that episode.

Usually he was noncommital. Usually it was screw you, take care of yourself, I'm not my brother's keeper. If you've got yourself in trouble, get yourself out. Don't bother me.

That night he was different, actually concerned. Almost as if he thought of me as a brother, along with Hank. As if he really did give a damn what happened to me.

He gave me a long lecture that night, for instance, on my eating habits. He said, "God damn it, I saw you the other night—you were eating in the Chinaman's joint up in the market."

I remembered. I was eating rice and peeled shrimp and vegetables—the Chinaman made it beautifully and I ate it all.

"You've got to stop eating that stuff, Jake," he said. "I

128

know you've been around a lot. But you and Hank may be cruising the world and visiting a hell of a lot of foreign places and you're going to run into a bug someday that'll kill you."

I wasn't arguing, I was listening, startled at how really serious he was about what I might be doing to myself. "You don't know what you're getting into, Jake. In places like that—don't ever drink the water, don't ever drink the milk, don't ever eat the vegetables." He said, "Christ, when I was in Africa I got the god-damnedest case of dysentery, and my guts were hanging out my asshole and I had to tuck them back in after every shit. *That* was god-damned annoying.

I appreciated the fact that he was telling me all this for my own good, but I contended that I was different. I'd built up an immunity to almost everything. "You have to understand, Stein—we used to go swimming in those goddam sluggish rivers in Iowa. All of us young guys. And one guy would take his safety pin and we'd all have boils, carbuncles, and each guy would get his turn with the pin and lance the boils and that way we'd get release and the swelling would go down. I've been vaccinating myself that way for years."

"Balls, Jake," he said. "That's Iowa; this is Cuba. They got different germs."

I said, "What do they do down here—speak Spanish?"

And he laughed and said, "Let's have another drink."

Stein, I learned, was really scared to death of bugs. He kept warning me that night about germs. I kept waiting for him to tell me about the dangers of the whores and VD. I

129

was going to tell him that he could talk all he wanted about my eating, but not about my fucking. But Stein had more sense than to get into that.

Another time, he talked about truth. This was his real hangup. You could steal, seduce, cheat, maybe worse. But don't lie. Live with the truth—on your own terms, maybe —but live with it. Truth was something you had to stay with, no matter what else you did. He told me that a lot of times.

He didn't believe in God but he believed in this. And he made it stick with the people around him. You just couldn't bullshit to hear yourself talk. If you said something, you had to stay with it or Stein would come driving in at you. "If you don't know what you're talking about— for Christ's sake, shut up."

On the boat once, some of the crowd, a couple of men, were arguing about getting laid and what was a good lay —how, when, which and why. They were really trying to sound as if they knew everything there was to know about servicing a broad. Stein was sitting nearby reading the newspaper and the guys went on talking and debating and sounding like real experts. Finally Stein looked up and said, "God damn it, neither one of you knows what you're talking about. A good lay takes four hours."

Then he went back to reading the newspaper.

Stein was a strange creature, pure animal, pure physical, but with that brilliant mind. And his timing was incredible —fists or phrases. He could destroy an antagonist equally with a smash to the jaw or a sentence of vitriol.

The individuals on whom he'd turn were the frauds and

130

the liars. For whatever reasons, he didn't put me in those categories.

But one night he did talk more directly about where I was going. Or at least he came closest to it.

We were together at a bar, one of those dark waterfront joints. This was the Four Brothers Bar, where the air was dank and the shadows cool and the beer was cold.

There was a silence between us. Since I knew Stein had been talking with Josey, I was being careful and holding my words.

It was Stein who broke the silence after a moment or two, in that abrupt way of his. "Jake—you can't win."

No answer from me.

Stein said, "It's one thing nobody can win. You can't beat the law."

Deep inside me, I knew he was right. All my life I'd been thinking I could beat it. And every time I tried to do something the hard way, I lost. I kept telling myself it wasn't because of *what* I did, good or bad. I kept thinking it was because I was a born loser.

He wasn't letting me off the hook. There were boundaries, he was saying. Lines beyond which you couldn't go safely, just as there are danger angles on a course you navigate between two hazards. You can't come too close to either. You have to clear both—safely.

But there were other things that he wasn't putting into words. I knew what they were. I couldn't belong in this circle in which I had somehow been accepted, the circle of Hemingway and his family and his achievements and his world-wide recognition and fame.

There was no order to leave, no wave of the hand pointing

to the door. That was neither threat nor promise. It was, in the peculiar way he had, simply a facing of realities as they were.

I could not continue leading two lives or using the glittering Hemingway world as a front.

I still felt that friendship existed between us, even the respect he had for me. I was a man in my own right. He accepted me still on these terms. The choice I faced was not put into words; I knew and Stein knew. It was simply a fact to be dealt with.

I blamed no one but myself. I felt my life had been shaped out of some distorted mold of my own making. I had lived by my wits too long; it was too deeply ingrained, ever since I stole my first breakfast bottle of milk from somebody's front porch.

There wasn't any way to win, not for me. Not that way. That was Ernest Hemingway talking, half loaded, sitting beside me and staring ahead at the shadows in the bar.

I was leery—even though she was leggy as all hell. I liked my freedom and I liked having money in my pocket. I could still remember the days when even the Cuban prostitutes wouldn't look at me. "Beesness is beesness," they would say in their thick Spanish accents, "and love is bool sheet."

A member of the consul's staff we hired knew all the ropes that had to be pulled if we wanted to get the *Golden Eagle* out of Cuban waters and over to Key West. He worked it all out by a devious legal approach: he got the carpenter who built the boat to certify that he never built it. "All you do is pay the carpenter twenty bucks and he'll swear to it, all right. Then we can export the boat as lumber—a bunch of lumber made up into a raft."

It sounded like a Cuban Alice in Wonderland, but never mind. That was how we worked it out. The Cuban courts and judges were delighted at the solution, because that would get two crazy American sailors—Hank and me—out of their hair.

Walking out of the courtroom I looked across the aisle, and who should I see but my friend and associate Pico with two men holding him. And Pico, seeing us, was crying out, "Jake, Jake, they're holding me *incomunicado*. . . ."

Well, it was a pretty funny thing in the courthouse corridor. Here was my underworld accomplice Pico being held by two strong-arm guards and he's yelling to me desperately to help him and to save him. The guards are trying to pull him away from us but we have our attorney with us, and he says, "Say, wait a minute. You can't do that to this gentleman—he's an American citizen."

I was really caught in the middle; there wasn't anything

I could say to Hank or the lawyer about Pico, good or bad. The lawyer was all up in arms that this could happen to an American citizen. "How long have they been holding you, Mr. Pico?" he demanded.

And Pico says, "Oh, for about two weeks. On no charge whatsoever except I had some papers on me for a big Sikorsky S38 amphibian airplane. They think the plane is here in Cuba and they're holding me on the mere suspicion that I know where it is in Cuba. It's an outrage."

The attorney agreed. He started action immediately in the courts, and since there was no evidence that anybody had brought a plane into Cuba, they let Pico go. As we were leaving the courtroom, Pico tipped me off as to where the plane really was—in an old, deserted World War I seaplane base a few miles north of Key West.

"It's mostly swamp now," Pico said, "but there are still ramps there, and you can take off a plane and bring it in."

I knew he was talking about a shuttle service he had talked about earlier, flying Chinese aliens in from Cuba and taking back guns and ammo for the revolutionaries.

About two weeks later Hank and I got the boat out and took her over to Key West. The manifest we had with us listed the craft as a raft of lumber.

For months we had been talking about our projected world-circling cruise on the *Golden Eagle*. Each time we'd start out, we'd come back to Havana. When we finally got to Key West this time, I said to him, "Hank, what are we gonna do now, you and I?"

I was waiting for him to say, "Now we start on the cruise," but Hank said, "Well, I just heard from Patsy."

135

Patsy was a beautiful girl who was close to his family. Hank had known her for many years, and loved her very deeply.

And he says, "I think I'll go up there, stay a little while in Chicago and see Patsy."

These words—"a little while up there"—struck hard in my mind. I said, "Hank, you're a liar. You're never coming back."

"No," he said. "I don't know. I mean—I think we may get married."

"In other words the trip around the world that you and I have been talking about all these months is over—*kaput* —all finished?"

He more or less admitted it then. This was a terrible blow to me. The big deal was off. The trip around the world was off.

For a little while I felt lost, really lost. The whole thing had come apart. There was nothing, nowhere to go. Stein was off somewhere; the marriage with Pauline was breaking up. Stein had met Martha Gellhorn one day in Sloppy Joe's bar and fallen for her. Hank was heading north to marry Patsy.

It was the end of the goddam tropical trolley.

That afternoon I disappeared from the usual haunts in Key West and went out to the deserted seaplane base. Sure enough, there was Pico. He had managed to get out of Cuba and there he was, working on this plane, getting it ready to fly.

I asked him what in hell he was doing now and he said he was still smuggling Chinese, and desperately needed help because it took two men to fly this plane.

Hank had blown the plans for our trip. Everybody else had walked out of my life. With nowhere else to go, I went to work again helping Pico put the plane into working operation. Of course, I'd never flown a plane and knew nothing about airplane engines whatsoever. But who cared about that?

I was back in this lousy business that I hated. I didn't know where we would be heading or who or what we would be carrying or whether we would wind up dead or alive. I only knew that an era of my life appeared to be ending.

Something new—more violent, more destructive—was about to begin.

## 20. Disaster in Mineola

Pico and I got the Sikorsky amphibian not only operationa
but flying smooth as a living bird. He took her up and dow
a couple of times and let me fly her and bring her in. Al
though I had never done it before, I seemed to be able t
pick up anything mechanical or anything that moved o
flew. Learning to handle the bird was no trick.

I wasn't a licensed pilot and had no right to be flying
a plane. But this was a good while back and the rules weren'
quite so tightly enforced. In any case, Pico was there too. I
was his gull. We made a couple of flights with the amphib
ian, at night, flying down to Cuba with a load of stuff. An
bringing back passengers.

We got them into the swamp and up on the ramps and
brought them at night over to the main road and the pickup
spot. At the pickup spot they were met by our men driving
jitney buses, the wildcat service that used to carry passengers between the third-rate hotels on their way up North.

When these men picked up our cargo of Chinese, they drove only at night, stopping during the daylight hours in secluded spots. A jitney full of Chinamen would look mighty strange careening along the highway in broad daylight.

We couldn't have lights on coming in or taking off, which made it dangerous and tricky getting in and out at night. Coming in one dark midnight, we knocked off a pontoon. We could have capsized except that we were in shoal water and couldn't actually have gone all the way over. I climbed out on the top of the wing and my weight was enough to straighten her out. Then Pico gunned her out and up onto the ramp.

The plane's engines were still operational, but they'd been shaken up in the minor crack-up, and to keep making these runs in the plane we had to have new Pratt and Whitney engines. The only place we could get that done was at Roosevelt Airfield, in Mineola, New York.

Pico and I flew up to Mineola to get new engines. But you couldn't just fly in, get the engines installed, and fly out. There were eight notches of speed ranges on the engines, and you had to break the engines in one notch at a time; the entire process took two days. This was the breaking-in period. And all of it had to be done on the ground. We went through all notches and the breaking-in process— it went on hour after hour, the noise roaring up louder and louder with each new level of RPMs. It was a shattering experience.

There was unfortunately another, even-more-shattering experience right in the middle of all that noise. Pico left me to sleep in and guard the plane at night. One morning I woke to a lot of noise outside the plane. About eight customs and internal revenue people had surrounded the plane and were standing guard with drawn guns, calling on me to surrender.

Pico at that particular moment wasn't anywhere in sight.

The chief customs man said they knew I had flown the plane in without a license. I said I hadn't flown it in; it was the owner of the plane who flew it in. I wasn't the owner, I explained.

They said, "Owner? Where is he? We've been watching you for a week. You're the only one who's been operating this thing. So far as we're concerned, you're it."

"I'm just a helper," I insisted. "Just a stooge. I can't fly a plane."

"We've got several people here," the customs man declared, "who say you flew this plane."

I said, "I was sitting in the copilot's seat but I wasn't flying."

"What the hell were you doing in the copilot's seat if you weren't flying it?" he demanded. "Or helping to fly it?"

"I was just up there for a better view."

We went inside one of the shacks on the field and sat down. They were watching me very closely.

They said, "Who was flying it?"

"The other guys were flying it."

There was a silence. Then one of the men asked, "What do you do?"

"I'm a sailor," I told them. "I like boats. I've been down South working around with boats. I was in Mobile for a time. Key West. Havana."

"Didn't you have a job of any kind? How could you live like that if you didn't have a job?"

I was damned upset right about then. And scared. All those warnings of Stein kept coming back, churning inside me. *You can't beat the law, Jake . . . there's no way to beat it . . . you can't win. . . .*

Without thinking clearly, almost without realizing what I was saying, I blurted out, "I wasn't broke. Hell, I was staying with the Hemingway family in Key West. Living down there and going out on their boat. I'm a friend of the Hemingway family. . . . I fished down there with him in the Gulf Stream. . . ."

A couple of the customs men looked at each other and one of them said to me, "You mean—Ernest Hemingway?"

I said yes. Then one of the men looked at the other and said, "And I'm Herman Melville. Who are you?"

I said, "No, it's true."

I remember thinking: If you tell the truth they don't believe you. You lie, they think it's the truth. I could see they didn't believe any of it. One of them eyed me very closely. "You mean you're talking about Ernest Hemingway, the writer?"

"Yeah—the writer."

The man said, "Mister, that's a crock of shit."

They were staring at me as if I were some kind of maniac. Finally one of them said, "Where were you before you were with the Hemingways?"

"Well, before that I was up in Mobile."

"What were you doing there?"

"I did odd jobs. Fooling around on boats. That was where I first met Hank Hemingway."

They seemed hardly to listen to me. One of them was on the phone putting in a call to Mobile. They found out from the records that I had had some connections there with questionable figures and I'd been picked up there but wasn't convicted of anything.

A third customs detective came in and one of the other men said to him, "Hey, Harry—you want to interrogate this drifter?"

I was incensed. I said, "What do you mean—me a drifter?"

Never before in my life had I thought of myself in that footloose term. But the detective said, "Well, now, what would you call yourself? Two weeks ago you were in Key West. Three weeks ago you were in Havana. A couple of years or so before that, you were in Mobile. . . ."

"Well, we have no record of any conviction against you," one of the other men said. "But there's one way we can clear up this whole thing real fast."

What they did was go into the next room and put in a call to Ernest Hemingway in Key West.

Of course, I didn't hear the conversation and they didn't give out any too much information as to what he had told them. But it was apparent he had confirmed what I said—that I had been living with the family and with his brother Hank Hemingway and that Hank and I had been cruising around Cuba in the sloop.

They didn't mention whether or not Stein told them about our abandoned plan to circumnavigate the globe.

Whatever else, this cleared me of being a liar about Stein. And of being a drifter with no roots or ties at all.

But when the detective said that about the drifter it was

the first time I'd ever really been confronted with myself.
My family always kept saying for me to settle down. They
thought of me as a lost cause. But I never thought of myself
as a drifter. I thought of myself as a really bright young
man who wanted to get a real taste of the world; the whole
fucking world was my private clambake.

They took me from Mineola, Long Island, in a car across
the East River, to the Custom House, in downtown Manhattan.

Funny thing. Years later, when my whole role in life
had changed and I turned honest, and was married and had
four children of my own, I went across that same bridge
over the river and the kids saw the spectacular sight of the
Empire State and the other buildings for the first time.

As we came in, that time, Sandy, my wife, was with us,
and the kids were exclaiming about the wonderful view and
I said, "Yes, it sure is, isn't it?" And I said, "You know, the
first time I saw this view, I had an armed detective guard-
ing me on each side in the back seat of the car.

They said, "What do you mean?"

I explained that I'd never come into New York before
and I didn't come in willingly that first time either. I was
brought into New York by the authorities.

Sandy was upset about this and she said, "Oh, Jake, why
do you have to bring that up now?"

I said, "Well, it's the truth. Why not tell them the story,
the truth?"

From there on into the city I related to the children what
had happened that day the customs people escorted me
into town.

They took me up to the top of the Custom House to talk

143

with the top man of the Immigration Department. The building is an odd kind of old-fashioned structure way downtown, and the windows at the top make it seem like some primitive suite in the Tower of London.

This top immigration official seemed greatly distressed about the situation and kept saying how he would appreciate it very much if I would help him out on something. He kept explaining how the plane I'd been on, the Sikorsky, had caused them all sorts of headaches.

"We've been chasing this damned thing all over the Florida Keys," the official said. "We chased it all the way up the coast to Mill Basin."

Mill Basin, in Canarsie, was our operating base in Brooklyn.

"Then all of a sudden it vanishes from Mill Basin," the official went on. "And we don't know where it's been. And then big as a balloon it shows up here in Mineola. Now, all we want to know is—what's happening? What's been going on here?"

Now he took on the fatherly tone. "Son," he said, "won't you try to help us out? This Sikorsky has been driving us nuts."

Then he went on very gently: "Did anything ever happen, son, while you were flying with this plane? Did anything or anybody ever do or say anything, or did you see anything, that might make you believe they were doing anything except flying passengers for hire?"

I said, "No, I certainly didn't see anything or hear talk of anything like that."

The official said, still very gently, "Well, they *were* doing something else, you know."

144

I said, "No! What? What were they doing?"

"They were flying in alien Chinese," he said. "Smuggling them illegally into the country."

I said, "Aliens? Alien Chinese? Hell, no. I wouldn't touch that stuff with a ten-foot pole. I'm a sailor and a fisherman and I like to try all kinds of transportation—planes, motor-boats, sailboats. I just hitched a ride up to New York in his plane. . . ."

They said, "Well, what are you doing, anyway, in New York? Do you know anybody in New York, anyone at all?"

"Well, the truth is," I said, "I'm heading home to Iowa, where I live, where my folks live, Mount Vernon, Iowa. I figured if I could get up here to New York it would be easier for me from here to get out there. All I'm trying to do is to go home."

He sat silent for a while, sort of thinking. Then he shook his head and said slowly, "Well, all right. I guess. But I wish, son, if you do know anything, you'd tell us."

It sounded so real, so sincere, the way he said that. For just a moment, my conscience bothered me. But then I forgot it. The truth was that they knew, or thought they knew, that I was a part of all this, at least far more than I had admitted. And it was true. I did know these people— Pico and Honest John—and I had worked with them.

The authorities decided to hold me, there in the Custom House, for more questioning, not on any charges but simply for investigation. But apparently they found nothing, and finally they let me go.

And the deputy immigration chief said, "Son, do you know where you're going now?"

"At this point," I told him honestly, "I have no idea. As I told you, this is the first time I've ever been in New York."

So he said, "You don't even know how to get out of here, do you? Well," he said, "you take the subway downstairs and you go up to Penn Station and take a train.

They asked me if I had any money and I said no, not one solitary cent. They said, "Well, we brought him in here. We'd better get him out."

So they took up a collection between the two of them— thirty-eight cents. Five for the subway and the rest for the fare to Elizabeth, New Jersey.

I had already told them about my early youth and how I'd learned to ride the freights. The man said, "From Elizabeth you can get your fast freight. You'll be home before you know it."

It didn't quite work out that way, for all their good intentions. I did get the subway uptown to Penn Station. I didn't even have a shirt on—only a leather jacket buttoned up to the neck. And I did get to New Jersey and hopped a freight. But riding this freight I began thinking about Pico. How does he know I might not talk? And Pico knows my home address.

So I didn't get off in Iowa. I went right on through to San Francisco and hung around there a couple of months, working a little on the docks. Then, one day when I figured it was safe, I drifted back to my home.

By the time I got back I was so tired I went to sleep on the sleeping porch, and my mother came out to see who it was. I scared hell out of her, because I heard the noise when she opened the porch door and in one second I was on my feet standing before her with a knife in my hand.

That was what my life to that point had taught me.

My mother thought I was a ghost, she was so startled to see me. She told me she hadn't believed she'd ever see me again—alive.

# II

## Jake and Hank

*I thought I had blown the whole bit with the Hemingways after that fiasco in Mineola.*

*The fact that Stein vouched for me to those customs people was a personal thing of vast importance to me. The fact that he would do it at all, knowing him. He could just as well have told them, "What do I know about it? You ask Jake himself. Not me."*

*I would not have blamed him, God knows. I knew Stein didn't want any kind of involvement like that. It could have splashed all over the papers. He didn't want to be involved; it touched him, it touched his special brand of posture and dignity.*

*I understood Stein, his reactions, even at a distance. I could catch his reaction even in a phone call I did not actually hear.*

*A breaking point had come. Stein was a dominating personality who really had little time for anyone but himself*

151

*and his work and his screwing. I had absorbed part of that personality; I found myself thinking in his patterns, talking in his way, parroting his words, even his style in violence.*

*The power that strides through almost all of his books also strode through most of his life, trampling down whatever got in his way. It was his need, his physical, intellectual, emotional need, to crush any antagonist, to plunge the blade into the charging bull, smash his fist into his opponent's face, or try four-hour adultery on the Pilar.*

*He was not easy to understand at any time. But one facet was clear; such a dominant individual could overwhelm those around him. He was the star, the center, the world, the universe. Despite himself. Despite the man of the people he tried and wanted to be. This was what his brother Hank was trying to emerge from. It was what I had also recognized.*

*My relationship with the Hemingways, to me, was one of the most significant facts of my life.*

*Now it was ended. The phone call from Mineola to Stein had rung off any further relationship. That was the way I read the situation.*

*But, as usual, I was wrong again.*

## 21. Chicago Gothic

I stayed only a few weeks with my family in Iowa, putting together the pieces, you might say.

En route east from Iowa, I stopped off in Chicago to see my brother John, the one who had changed the spelling of our name to the Greek version, Klima, and who was achieving quite a musical reputation as bass violinist in the Chicago Symphony. I visited with him and several other pals I had in Chicago, and then I heard through someone that Hank Hemingway was working on the Chicago *News*.

I hadn't seen him for more than a year, but, after all, we had been together in and around Cuba for a couple of years of our lives. I called him to say hello.

Hank was really great. We got together and had a few drinks and talked about the past. Hank said, "Look, Jake, we've got that big house in Oak Park. It's got more rooms than we know what to do with. Why don't you stay out there with us? It'll be like old times, Jake. Chicago's not Havana, but there are afterhours places."

Since I hadn't had any idea of exactly where I would stay, and didn't want to barge in on John's quarters, I said I'd be very grateful. Hank had to get back to work, but he told me to go right out there.

He'd be there after his stint in the city room.

I went out alone to Oak Park.

It was an old-fashioned, looming, gingerbread house, set back from the street, a big, gloomy place you could rattle around in for months. I felt out of place with my luggage in hand as I walked the long path to the front door.

But I didn't realize the jolt I was in for. I rang the bell and waited. After some seconds, I heard footsteps. The door opened.

I'll never forget that moment. The person standing there was tall and wore a long, old-fashioned dress. But it was not, in any real sense, what I expected. This was Stein standing before me, in woman's clothes. It was his face, his body, his features.

It was, in fact, Gracie—Mrs. Hemingway. She could have been the actual twin of her own son. It was uncanny, frightening. I almost expected to hear his voice, his laughter.

But there was only the lady standing before me with her own society-shaped dignity and, I realized, her self-sufficiency. She needed no one else.

Her costume was something out of the past, as if she was making a special stand of clinging to past styles and dress. I noticed also her incredible old-fashioned high-laced shoes.

154

I remember glancing at them and thinking, god damn, there must be buttons on those shoes. I remembered as a boy of five or six that women wore shoes with buttons; most shoes had buttons then. I remember fighting the buttonhook getting my own shoes on.

Anyway, I was wrong about Mrs. Hemingway's shoes, because they were laced; they were very high, white, laced shoes.

Mrs. Hemingway was a big woman, a big-busted woman with wide shoulders and a very florid face. A good-looking woman, she had pride and character. But the shock of seeing the image of her son standing before me in long, old-fashioned skirts just bowled me over.

She was gracious although she was not expecting me. Although Hank had given me the address and telephone number, I hadn't had sense enough to call her in advance and explain about Hank's invitation. But when I told her who I was, she was delighted. That was when she told me about Stein's letter regarding me and Hank.

I came to know her well in the couple of weeks I stayed at the Oak Park house. I could recognize her varying attitudes, the disinterest she had toward her children—most of all, it seemed to me, toward Stein. I understood how Hank and Stein felt as they did. Children always reject their parents in some measure. I did, with my own mother. Looking back, perhaps I was the luckiest; perhaps I had the least reason for rejecting my mother. Much as she tried to drive me into the grooves, she had not, in her zeal, driven my father to blow out his brains.

During the various stages with Stein in Havana, I heard him say a number of times that one day he was going

155

to write what he called only "the big book." He never described it in any other way, nor did he give any hint of what it would be. But there is no doubt in my mind as to what it was, not since the first moment I had a view of his mother. It would be about her, about the family, about patterns straight out of the tragedy of Hemingway's own life.

When I read his *A Moveable Feast,* I was struck between the horns with his account of Hadley. There were times when I was critical of Stein for his marital game of musical chairs—and wives.

Stein was married to Pauline when I first met him. He had come to realize how she had deliberately and coldly broken up his marriage with her former roommate, Hadley, in order to marry him herself. And he had been damned fool enough to let her do it.

Reading *A Moveable Feast,* knowing many of the people involved, I realized that Stein had made a tragic mistake in letting Pauline destroy his marriage with Hadley. He had been poor with her, he had suffered a lot of deprivations, but he had written and written well, and he had been happy.

Pauline came along dripping money and position and offering an easy avenue, and for these Stein threw away one of the real things in his life—Hadley. Later, as his writing in *A Moveable Feast* reveals, he recognized he had muffed it, had made a mistake and there was no way of restoring what was finished. Hadley was happily married again, as Stein went back to her himself personally to verify.

He had been wrong, and in the end he realized this, and

eing the basically honest man he was, he said so in *A Moveable Feast*.

Having known Pauline and seen her and Stein together many times, I can understand now how Pauline took over. was his greatest mistake. I am grateful for his having admitted this in print.

Over many years I have been in a kind of dilemma, wondering how and why I could admire Stein so much and at the same time feel such anger at his rejection of Hadley in favor of Pauline's rich-bitch syndrome.

I see him now in a different perspective: A man frantic, lashing out at others, and seeing in them the big mistake he had made. That was why he had slugged Pauline's rich friend over the ten-dollar tip. Stein felt silly about that the next day; he knew it wasn't the rich guy's fault, but his own. It had been his choice between Hadley and Pauline. He had allowed Pauline to take over. After that, there was nothing to change it. Nothing.

All of this would have been part of the big book he never wrote. Perhaps it might have been called *Women Without Men*.

His mother would have been the central character; she would have been the old woman of the Oak Park mansion; he would have been a focal point of to have and reject.

I could be wrong as hell, but I doubt it. The story would be built around the matriarchy of Mrs. Hemingway, the world of Stein and Hank and the daughters, the contrast of humanity and aloofness that were Gracie and Clarence Hemingway, against the patterns of prestige, society, the surface calms and the underlying storms and self-destruction and death.

And through it all, the sometimes loving, sometimes uncaring, sometimes blighting hand of Gracie Hemingway—proud of her world-famous son for being world famous, and embarrassed as hell, although she would not say it publicly, by his frankness in the books regarding sex and by his use of language, particularly in that era, that did not go with Oak Park drawing rooms.

Once, we were talking in the late afternoon. I was waiting for Hank to come in; we were going out that night with some people he knew. His mother was working on a painting—one of the Mexican scenes—and I was admiring it, and she broke in, just once, for the first and only time in this tone or approach, and said, "I assume my son is quite happy in his world down there."

In just those words, those tones. I said, "Oh, sure. He's as happy as anyone can be who seems to be driven the way he is. He drives himself, especially when he writes."

I remember she didn't anwer me after that but kept looking at the picture *she* had painted. Then she carried it into the other room and went on about whatever she was doing.

Seeing her, meeting her, talking with her, I came to understand some of Stein's character I did not understand before. His innate acceptance of civilization, his rebellion against much of the establishment he innately had to support. His unwillingness to surrender independence and yet his ties with those of the past or present. Stein, of course, always tried to get rid of his money; he rarely had any with him and he once indicated to me that he didn't want to have money, that he liked to spend it drinking, giving big parties, fishing, doing anything to get rid of it pleasantly—his idea was to be broke so he felt he had to write. This was the contradiction of the soul.

One time he got rid of a large chunk of dough by the unique approach of giving it to his immediate relatives. On that occasion, as I was told by Stein and by Hank, he gave his mother forty thousand dollars and his sisters and brothers ten thousand dollars each. (These sums were approximately four or five times what the same amount would purchase four or five decades later.)

After this act of beneficence, Stein told his beneficiaries, "Now, don't any of you ask me for any money for any reason whatever as long as you live. I'm giving you this outright. But don't anybody ask me for a cent again or a loan or anything else."

This was his own, immediate family.

The fount of all this, the mother-image heroine of the big book Stein never wrote, rides through all of this in her unperturbable way. She was doing oil paintings—in fact, the first day I met her she was at work on one in the Oak Park house.

I was amazed at how good she was. Just back from Mexico—she had driven down there and back herself—she had a lot of sketches and rough paintings that she was finishing of adobe huts and blue western skies, bright sun and shadows.

They were good pictures, not unlike the stuff Maxwell Parrish used to do. I was surprised at how skillfully she used the blues and browns.

She did travel a lot, and she lectured at various women's clubs about art and culture. The interpretation of life, I suppose you could call it. But from what I could learn, she spoke practically not at all about her son Ernest Hemingway.

Her attitude about him, in fact, startled me at first, the first days I was in that Oak Park house of shadows. We would talk little trivialities or about her paintings or almost anything at hand, and I would bring in Stein in one way or another and she would almost brush it aside. Or it would be "Oh, yes. I'm sure he is getting along fine." And that was practically it.

It was not a mother's concern for her son, whatever it may have been. I've known mothers who ask how is the dear boy and is he eating enough and has he been sick and please tell him to take care of himself and to write. Quite the opposite reaction came from Mrs. Hemingway. It almost seemed like a duty she was going through to say anything about him at all. As far as I can recall, she did not once mention anything at all about Stein's writing.

This is why I say Stein was the perfect combination of his parents—the loving, outgoing man who was his father, and the creative, self-centered, carefully programed lady who was his mother.

I'm saying some of these things probably without any right to say them, because I didn't know the family that intimately. But my role gave me a certain right, because I was able to see the family—his mother, for instance—objectively. I was on the outside, not involved in any of their passionate arguments and debates and hates. Everybody involved had long since chosen up sides, especially in the suicide of Stein's father.

I was the fly on the wall looking at these characters. And

160

all I really knew was that none of this family were happy, including Gracie, and above all her son Ernest, despite all his laughter and lust for life, his booze and his ladies. And all his fame.

I am convinced this was the material out of which Stein wanted to shape "the big book" he would one day write.

But again speaking as the impartial fly, I wonder if he could have written it, if perhaps it would have been too damned close to his guts.

Even Stein, even before his final illness, might not have been able to take the drain and agony of reliving that Oak Park soap opera all over again.

## 22.  Kaleidoscope

It was a period of transition from early youth to something else—something closer to adulthood. But not yet mature. It was still helter-skelter activities, shifting patterns, one minute to the next. The events themselves constantly changing. They become blurred in your mind. Yet some of the episodes of that era were burned into our erotic, sometimes stupid, young brains. . . .

My travels after I left Chicago for New York taught me one thing I had to deal with—if I really wanted to make any kind of mark, I had to get myself more education. I knew only one place where I could live at minimum expense and get additional education—Cornell College, back in my Mount Vernon, Iowa, home.

Cornell accepted me. My parents were leading citizens of the town; my father was on the school board. Great as it was educationally, the college was one of those Midwestern institutions that could drive a grown man out of his bird. It was, for example, strictly beerless and smokeless. And stringently sexless.

Since I was a little older than most guys, I was used to other ways of living. I was still going to get educated at this college. But living on campus was not the way. I and another fellow who was studying there took an apartment just off the college grounds. As a symbol of our basic liberation, we got ourselves a milk cooler and filled it full of five gallons of gin.

The apartment operation proved slightly unorthodox, and only my father's reputation for propriety saved us from serious disciplinary action after numerous reports of outré parties in our rooms filtered back to the dean. But we were ordered to give up the apartment and find other quarters.

As it happened, I had struck up a friendship with a young lady who taught at the college. She had her own home and lived alone. I could move in anytime I wanted. I told the college people I was staying temporarily in a shack down by Cedar River. Then I moved in with this teacher. It was a happy relationship for both of us. Unlike Stein, I had no wife about to barge in from Key West.

By a twist of bad luck, my father learned what was going on. He insisted I do something about it at once. If people saw me going in and out of that house at night, what would they think?

I didn't know, but I agreed to change things around. After that, I came in much later at night, when the rest of the community were presumably asleep.

This girl—I'm not sure I can remember her name—was happy with our warm and friendly relationship. I had a place to go while I was improving my educational background preparatory to making something of myself. My parents were content in the notion that I was staying at the Cedar River shack. The girl was just content. No one was hurt.

She ultimately went to New York, and I had to find new quarters. At some Beekman Place cocktail party, she heard people complaining that there were no more he-men on the stage, especially in off-Broadway shows.

She told them they were all crazy; she knew a real he-man. I was it. The next thing I knew, I had an offer from her to come East, all expenses paid, and become leading man in a theatrical venture in Milford, Connecticut.

This sounded like a new career. I headed for New York, where I could stay with my brother the sculptor. He was working at that time with Salvador Dali. Later, he worked with Malvina Hoffman. My brother knew dozens of girls in New York and we had a real living ball night after night.

My trouble here was—to put it simply—I hated the stage, hated acting, hated all the phonies I met in the theater. All I wanted to do was to get back to the one real world I loved —the sea.

There was one really good piece of news during this period. Hank and his wife had had a baby son. They named him Jake—in honor of me!

Hank, meanwhile, had also landed a new job as one of the editors on *Country Life*, within a few months would be working out of their New York office. Patsy, his wife, had to make arrangements to move East, and Hank had to find them living quarters first. She didn't know where she and little Jake could stay until this was all worked out. Hank got in touch with me and I found the solution by writing my parents in Mount Vernon, asking if Patsy and Jake could stay with them until Hank got relocated in New York.

It was all pretty complicated, of course, but my parents were delighted to have her and her son with them "as long as they want to stay."

I was with that great adventure in histronics in Milford, Connecticut, for about six months. I got to loathe the whole thing—the people, the parties, the women, even the martinis.

One day I had a call from Hank. He had a few weeks off and wanted me to go with him, Patsy, and little Jake on a cruise on the *Golden Eagle* from Key West to Yucatán, Mexico. Would I go as his mate?

It took me back a long while. And I was sure as hell ready to go.

Schedules and events and sequences get blurred. So many things happen; do we have them in proper order? Or does one have to worry so much?

Hank and I went down to Key West ahead of time to get things squared away. There were things wrong with the *Golden Eagle;* one of the masts looked as though it was eaten at the base with termites. I insisted on rigging a backstay before I would agree to go out.

The sloop was finally ready for the run across to Yucatán. Patsy and Jake arrived—he was two years old then—and we got underway. Once outside the Key West harbor we ran into heavy weather. Dark skies, high waves, heavy seas. We ran with reefed mainsail for two days. The morning of the third day, I looked at Patsy across the cockpit and I said, "Patsy, you're green. What the hell is the matter with you?"

"Jake," she said, "I'm pregnant."

"You're telling me you *know* you're pregnant?"

"Yes, Jake. I know."

I ran down into the cabin and told Hank. I raised hell with him about it, bringing a pregnant woman out on a cruise like this. But, of course, Hank hadn't known.

That didn't change the danger factor. I said, "Christ, Hank. She could miscarry. We've got to get her out of here fast, out of all this."

I knew our approximate position—just about twenty miles off the northwest tip of Cuba. There was a little town close to the point called La Fe. A hole in the middle of nowhere with a main street that looked like a tropical version of a wild-west movie set.

When I'd been bringing in guns and ammo I'd been into that village a hundred times. "We've got to get our asses out of this blow and into the harbor," I told Hank.

It took doing, but we got the *Golden Eagle* inside the harbor at La Fe. From there, Hank, Patsy, and Jake were able to go overland through Pinar del Rio back to Havana, where they got the ferry across the straits to Florida and Key West.

I stayed there with the *Eagle* in La Fe. It was no hardship. La Fe had a couple of bars and people who like to whoop things up because there is nothing else to do. They even had some *señoritas* hanging around with time on their hands. It was a real pleasant tropical rest period. About three weeks later, Hank arrived back in La Fe after having taken his pregnant wife and his son back to Chicago. We brought the craft safely back from its truncated cruise. Patsy later had her second child safely—another boy.

Patterns change. Even while we're looking, they change. One thing becomes something else.

Somewhere in Greenwich Village Hank went to a cocktail party. One of the girls at the party was a woman editor who happened to be working on *Country Life,* where Hank was also working. On the side, this editor was trying to help out on a weekly newspaper in Brooklyn Heights, across the river from Manhattan.

"What the paper needs," she told Hank, "is a real editor. I can't give it the time it needs. You know anybody might like to take a shot at it?"

Hank, who'd had a drink or two and was feeling nostalgic, remembered his old-time buddy, Jake Klimo. "Listen," he told her, "I think I've got your man."

He began to tell her about me and my various capabilities. The fact that I never edited anything before seemed unimportant to all of them. And nobody bothered to tell me. "He sounds great," they said. "Let's get him."

The next thing I knew I had a message from Hank informing me I had an offer for a job as editor of a newspaper in Brooklyn Heights. Along with this office, I learned later, I would have available as a part-time reporter a young girl whose name was Sandy.

I took the job because I needed it, not because I thought I knew what I was doing. But I started right off trying to build it up into an interesting paper by finding stories and features that seemed to have some excitement and weren't just junk nobody gave a shit about anyway.

167

I was doing pretty well on this editor job. We even gained on circulation and got a few ads. But the big thing about this job was running into this girl reporter named Sandy.

Naturally I met and was working closely with her. She was a damned good reporter and wrote damned good copy. But there was something else about her, too.

I kept looking at her and realizing she was beautiful; she was the best-looking girl I'd ever seen. And one of the loveliest I'd ever known.

This one really had me frightened. Because she was a woman like all women. She'd be trying to tame me and civilize me and make me all the things I'd been running from all my life.

Things inside me were churning. I had to get away. I had to find my way back to the sea.


On one of my trips South, I ran over to Key West to see if any of my friends, any of the old pirates, were doing anything interesting.

I was walking along, and suddenly I saw Stein coming up the street on the other side. He was in his shorts and barefoot and his shirt was open and he was carrying some books under his arm. Stein always walked on the balls of his feet, like an Indian or a cat. It was a strange walk but not affected. He told me once it had developed from all his years of fighting and sparring.

I hadn't seen or talked to Stein for a long long time. I wanted to see him, to talk to him. But I didn't want to embarrass him. I wouldn't turn off or look away. Maybe he'd remain preoccupied with his thoughts. Or would turn away himself.

Of course, he didn't. He looked over and saw me and he called out loud and clear, "Hey, come here. Come over here, Jake."

That time it was an order. I came across the street to where he was standing and I said, "Hi, Stein."

He said, "You son-of-a-bitch—what've you been doing? What were you doing that day in Mineola?"

It was a long time back—but it was right there on top.

I tried to explain that I knew I shouldn't have used his name, that it was just blurted out, I guess, because I was trapped. I said, "They called you? Didn't they call you?"

He said, "Listen, Jake. Don't you ever do that to me again. Ever." He paused, and then he said, "I lied to get you off the hook, to get you out of that jam. I told them you were with me all the time that year, but I lied. You were away a lot of the time and nobody, not even Hank, knew where the hell you were or what you were doing. I lied for you, Jake. But I'll never do it again. Remember that."

I said, "Jesus Christ, Stein. Whatever else I did wrong— I want to thank you for what you did."

I didn't know what else to say. There was no way of really thanking Stein; he had done what he decided he had to do—even against his better jugment. Even against all his goddam basic morality.

But just as suddenly, there in the Florida sun, his whole manner changed. "Okay, Jake," he said, "I had to get it off my chest. Let's go in and have a drink. How about it?"

We went inside the bar and had a few drinks and he asked about my plans and I told him I was riding pretty high.

He was grinning and not too upset, but he said, "You're a liar. You're in the business again."

I thought he meant smuggling in Chinamen and I said no, nothing like that. Stein seemed satisfied. He said he heard about me occasionally through Hank. He was always glad to see me: "Any time, Jake."

I still didn't know what I wanted to do with my life—except for that urge to go to sea. And after I met Sandy and realized how strongly I felt about her I knew that I had to get away. Sandy was too much, too charming, too beautiful. I wasn't built for marriage; I'd run from it for years. It was too late to change.

A few weeks later I walked along the East River, and at Thirty-fourth Street and the river was a garbage dump, and tied up there was an absolutely magnificent three-masted schooner, over a hundred and fifty feet long. She had a shiny black hull, high soaring masts and rigging. She was a real dream boat.

I stood there looking at her, and out comes an old friend of mine from days past in Cuba—wearing the same hat and spats and the goatee—Honest John. He goddam near fell overside in surprise. Down in the cabin was another old friend, he told me—Pico.

"The man who owns this boat has a plan to charter her out to us. We've got another man involved with us—Simpson. He's down in the cabin with Pico. We have plans to take her to South America."

170

Not what he said, but his tone, told me this was a lot more than just a boat ride. This was business.

The way I saw it then, with Sandy's face before me in my mind almost all the time, going away was my last shot at freedom. I started asking questions. Honest John said, "Not here. Let's go below. We can use you on this run, Jake."

As he started down the ladder to the cabin, Honest John said, "How's Hemingway, Jake? You see him any more?"

## 23.  Destination: Nowhere

It was strange how Stein—even off somewhere in France or Spain or wherever—seemed to cling to my being. Even at the East River garbage dump at Thirty-fourth Street, looking at that beamy, towering three-masted schooner. And talking again to Honest John.

I was back again, back in a role I had lived before.

Sure, I lived it, too, down there. We smuggled Chinamen in and carried booze in, and we even carried in pineapple tips and roots, which were illegal to export from Cuba because the Cuban Government wanted to keep a monopoly on the pineapple crops. I knew these people. I had lived some of that agony Stein wrote about.

Particularly in the Key West and Cuban period, Stein's world and mine merged and blended and grew confused. What was real and what was fiction became blurred— what was to Stein the story, underlying character and meaning, and what was to me the reality and the living and the peril.

172

In that sense I and people I knew belonged with Stein's characters. We were his goddam characters. And the group also included himself. We were all fragmentations of his world—the Harrys, the Margots, and other of his characters, as well as the Jakes, the Steins.

I went down the hatchway ladder to the cabin, where Honest John's pal Simpson was waiting to talk to me about a cruise to South America carrying a cargo of guns, ammunition, and high-grade dynamite.

God knows, if there were ever two characters out of a Hemingway story, it was these two men involved in this cruise. Honest John Cabarra, with his big, white, pointed mustache and his white, waxed goatee and his round beaver hat, looked like a Spanish grandee on hand either for a wedding or a wake.

Simpson, his pal, was something else. Honest John was a great guy who knew every crook and scoundrel in the Caribbean. But Simpson was an ugly asshole. Old Simpson was a beetle-browed, thin-faced, mean son-of-a-bitch. Well past sixty, Australian. He used to be on the grain runs, the big square-rigged grain clippers plying between Australia and England. Simpson talked Australian with a German accent; his people had emigrated originally from Germany.

There in the cabin, Simpson gave me the pitch. The guy who owned her was willing to charter her to us—no questions asked—provided we could get his automobile on board and take him and the car as far as Jacksonville, which was all right with Simpson and the rest of us.

Simpson knew he had to have a mate, somebody who could handle a ship. He looked me over with his squinting eyes as if I were something that dropped in from outer space. John and Pico had gone off somewhere by then. Simpson and I were alone.

He said, "You know Honest John long?"

I said, "Yeah."

"You worked with him?"

"Sure. He must have told you."

When you're in this kind of deal, you don't talk much; you don't say things straight out. Everything is understood. I knew he was just testing. He had all the facts he needed about me already.

He said, "Well, I'll tell you what we're doing. We're waiting here. We got to get a load of coal—and now there's a coal strike."

"And the other stuff?"

"That'll be in wooden cases—it'll go as boxes of books. But you can't just carry cases like that. We got to have coal on top. We can't go without coal and they aren't loading coal. So we're waiting."

The coal, of course, would be a cover cargo. The boxes of books that were, in fact, holding the ammo, dynamite, and machine guns, would be underneath the coal, in the hold.

The book deal was really hot—one of the shipping clerks in a major book firm of that day was working for the job. Boxes and phoney invoices supposedly for shipments of religious and educational books "for the dear sisters in the mission" were a cover for the guns and bullets and explosives to be shipped to South American rebels.

That shipping clerk was a real operator. He was dummying up manifests and shipping records and bills so confusingly no one could ever figure what we were doing. Basically, the story was supposed to be that we were carrying coal to Portugal. If anybody spotted the cases en route, our story was that we were taking books to the Maryknoll Sisters in Portugal. Fine old bindings for the convent. Bibles. Textbooks. Later we'd say the wind blew us off course, so instead of going to Portugal, we were driven down to South America.

I asked Simpson, "Exactly where are we planning to get blown to?"

He named a South American port on the northwest coast.

So we waited for the coal strike to get over. We waited three weeks. I even brought over Sandy—whom I was trying to forget—to see this beautiful schooner I was on.

Simpson had gotten rid of the whole crew and he was glad to have me along because it was hard to get a real sailor and he was hurting for somebody to keep the ship in shape. As soon as I came on I began rigging her—I rerigged the whole ship. Her running rigging was getting pretty rotten.

Finally we worked it all out so that we could leave, coal or not. Simpson and I and a couple of hands for the galley and the lines would bring her down to Jacksonville, Florida, and Honest John would pick us up there. Instead of coal, we'd get lumber as a cover cargo in Jacksonville. The other stuff—the "books"—we'd ship down to Jacksonville by truck and load on board there.

We picked up lumber in Jacksonville on consignment; we could always sell it somewhere. Pico left us here. He was the gun connection and had other fish to fry. We got dock space at Commodore's Point and began loading at night, stowing the cases of "books" in the hold with the lumber. Nobody got suspicious.

That was the cargo we took to Venezuela.

It was one hell of a trip, one hell of a cruise. Everything was done by hand: raising sail—even the anchor was hoisted by hand. It took hours to raise the ten thousand square feet of sail on the three masts, but once we got it all aloft, we sailed like sons-of-bitches.

We had to get this stuff in to the beach by night. The beach itself was deserted and stark and flush up against the high mountains on the South American coast. The mountains plunged straight down into the sea. There was hardly any beach. The revolutionaries would come down the mountain trails under cover of dark and take the ammo and the dynamite and machine guns up the trails in the dark on the backs of the burros.

We laid off a long way doing this—out of sight of the customs people and the army guards that always kept up their patrols. We'd unload into the small double-ended whaleboats we carried. We had extra oars under the thwarts of these boats, because we would break or lose our oars riding the huge breakers in.

The whaleboats had a six-man crew, one man in the bow, four amidships rowing, and another at the stern with a big sixteen-foot sweep oar we used as a rudder. It was absolutely imperative that you keep the whaler crosswise to the seas.

In the darkness, in those whaleboats, you wait, just outside the breakers. Nobody talks as you wait, counting the waves coming in under you. The crew is counting, too; it's their lives as much as yours. You have to stay out there for maybe half an hour or longer just to get the feel of that sea. The trick, the whole trick, is sitting outside and waiting for the big one that will take you in.

Down there they had a special sequence of waves you had to get used to. There are seven surface waves and three subterranean waves. You go in on the last of those three underwater waves—that's the big one that carries you in. But you have to keep count, because the subterranean ones come in at different times, intermingled with the seven on the surface. I talked to a physicist, Jack Livingood, about this years later, and he got all excited and made me describe it in detail and took notes. He said this had to do with the wobbling of the poles, and it was only a theory people were still trying to prove, and what I reported might help establish this unusual variation of patterns in the ocean swells.

I told Jack that I was happy to be of some help to science but that I wore out a couple of assholes sitting out there in the dark all that time, trip after trip, getting the stuff in to the beach and waiting for those seas, counting those goddam seas. Once you know you have the big one, the granddaddy, you cry out, "Yo!" and we all start rowing like a bastard. You have to keep the boat right on the crest; you can feel it if you go too far forward—the oarsmen have to row backward then to keep her on top. You're going at an incredible speed in to the beach, on the top at thirty or forty knots. They put the speed of the water, when it tumbles as the wave breaks, at fifty knots or better.

All the time—and we had to make the run in to the beach

177

many times during the darkness to get the stuff in—you have to watch not to broach, because if you do you're dead. As the breaker lands the boat high on the beach, everyone throws down his oars, jumps over the side, and helps keep the boat heading forward, pushing and pulling the whaler higher up on the shore. All of this in total darkness and silence. Then the stuff is unloaded and put on the burros by the revolutionaries for delivery up the mountain.

We went in, of course, in the dark of the moon. But that mountain is a beautiful sight anyway as you're coming in. You see no lights, but you can see the mountain's huge silhouette against the sky and the stars.

We made ten trips like that, from the schooner to the beach and back, on the first night. We couldn't do more, because we had to pull out beyond twelve miles before it was dawn. Then we'd come back the next night. Altogether, it would take a week.

It was rough and really dangerous; how dangerous, I was about to learn. But there was pie to cut up at the other end; my cut for this trip, along with Honest John and Simpson, would be forty thousand dollars.

But we still had to get stuff ashore—and get out rapidly. There were government patrols in the mountains, hunting gunrunners. Patrols were out day and night.

A patrol caught the last burro train.

That was the beginning of trouble. An ex-sailor who happened to be on the patrol high on the mountain spotted our ship twelve miles out. They had gunboats to track us down. These gunboats tailed us for two days. Finally they tried to fire across our bow, but ripped our jib. It didn't matter.

Government boats closed in on all sides. There was nothing to do but heave to and surrender. Thank Christ we had landed all the stuff. They confiscated the schooner and threw the three of us in jail—about the worst jail I was ever in. It was in an old fort right on the waterfront. When the tide came in, it came to a height of about six inches in my cell. I couldn't sit down until it went out; I didn't want to rot my body sitting in the scum of that water in the cell. I used to hold my urine until the tide started out, so when it went out the urine wouldn't be in the cell. Jesus Christ, it was awful.

Every week, they took Simpson and me to the American consul general. The first time he saw us he was sitting with his feet on the desk. He said, "Well, they finally got you."

I said, "What do you mean?"

He says, "You've caused us enough trouble between Cuba and here. I'm awfully glad they caught you." Then he said, "What are you getting to eat?"

I said, "Christ, it's awful. A handful of beans and a handful of rice."

"Well, that's all right," the consul said. "That's in full accord with international law."

"But the beans aren't cooked."

"The rules don't say anything about cooking."

"But I'm in a bare cell," I persisted. "How can I cook in a prison cell?"

"Oh, you could grind them up if you wanted to."

Then he started in about the schooner and asked me, "Why aren't you sailing under the American flag?"

I said it was cheaper under the Honduran.

179

He said, "Why don't you get under the American flag—maybe I could give you some protection."

I said, "But I'm an American citizen."

"That doesn't make any difference—you're sailing under another flag."

Then I started to tell him about the treatment from the prison guards, who were really murderers. I said, "They're trying to kill me. They're going to kill me."

He was sitting there with his feet still on the desk and he was smiling at me and he said, "That's all right. They probably will. Forget it."

But I didn't, because I knew they would kill me if I stayed much longer.

I stood this about three months. I'd lost some sixty pounds. I looked and felt like someone in a horror film. One day when they were taking Simpson and me to our regular weekly visit to the American consul—international law demands this—I noticed that we had a new driver in the taxi that was taking us and the two guards who went with us. They told the driver to go to the *Consulado Norte-americano*. But I noticed that he was heading the wrong way; he was taking us not to the consulate, but to the American embassy.

Now, it happened the embassy was throwing a lawn party—the kind Hank Hemingway and I used to go to sometimes in Havana. Men in striped trousers, and tall, lovely dames.

Getting inside the embassy is a lot different from being at the consul's office. At the embassy you're on American territory. I took one look and I nudged Simpson. Then I reached in my pocket to get my seaman's book. As we pulled into the driveway, two sentinels stepped up and I gave Simpson a terrific jab. I went out one side of the cab and Simpson went out the other. One of us had a chance of making it.

The sentinels drew their guns. But I was holding my hand high and showing them and all the other marines around that I was holding this paper, this seaman's book, which had the American eagle insignia on it—the shield of the United States on it. I'm holding this up and yelling, "I'm an American. I'm an American."

And I'm running like all hell right for that high-society lawn party.

The two guards who had been with us caught Simpson before he could get inside the embassy grounds, but the guards didn't get me. I got inside. The marines, of course, surrounded me.

We just about broke up the lawn party completely. All the striped pants and lovely ladies were standing around gaping at me. I was a real wreck. I had on a ragged pair of pants, held up by a piece of rope. My shirt was torn. My hair was all the way down to my shoulders, and my beard was down to my chest. I looked like hell itself.

I kept saying, "Where's the ambassador?" And I kept hollering, "I'm from Iowa."

And I said "Iowa" so it sounded like "Ohio," which I had heard was where the ambassador came from.

When I got to him finally, he was staring at me and I played it straight and hard and I said, "These people are trying to kill me. Unless you help me I'm going to be murdered."

The ambassador seemed to have been given some hint

181

already as to the background of the story. "I've heard you were one of those men on the schooner they pulled in?"

I said yes, I was. He said, "Yes, I heard about you. But you were supplying German submarines."

"German submarines?" I almost blew my top at that. "How could we?" I asked him. "What kind of facilities do we have for that?"

"They say you were supplying them oil in drums."

I realized then, what had happened. On board, we had had about a hundred and fifty drums, hermetically sealed. They were drums full of water. Drinking water—spare water. We didn't want to take a chance on running short on that long cruise, never knowing what kind of foul water we would run into in local ports.

This was our supply. But someone had given the story out that the drums had diesel oil in them. And what were we doing carrying a hundred and fifty drums of diesel oil with no diesel engine on board?

I didn't know until that moment that this was the charge on which we were being held—without trial, without interrogation, without any hint of what they were accusing us of.

I told him, "If you take the trouble to examine what's in those drums, you'll find out they're as clean as this table top. They've never had oil in them—only water. Clean water."

Then I added, "Who told you that story? The consul general?"

The ambassador said, "Yes."

I knew there was a schism between the ambassadors, who are appointed diplomats, and the consuls, who were

182

career men. They mostly hated each other's guts. I learned this while I was hiding out in that consulate in Cuba; the consul and I talked about it, all the striped-pants backbiting. State Department crap.

I played this up a little to the ambassador in the garden, how the consul general wouldn't lift a hand to keep me from being destroyed. I didn't mention that the consul general's files showed me as a suspected gunrunner. I told him what I was going through in that jail, dying in its filth and rot and stench. And here I was, a poor Iowa youth trying to sell some lumber. I said, "Mr. Ambassador, you can go down personally and look at those barrels and see how miserable and fabricated that story they told you really is."

He says, "Well, I'll check on this. But in the meantime you'll have to go back to that jail."

I said, "All right—you send me back to that jail. But if you don't get me out of there, you're sending me to my death."

Everybody at the party was standing there. It was real-life drama and they were all listening.

The ambassador said, "I give you my word. If what you say is true and I find there is no proof—and I will look into it myself—I'll see you're freed.

I said, "Well, you'd better, sir. Because if you don't, the way they are treating me, I can't make it out alone."

I was taken back to the jail and lounged in that hellhole for another few days. Then I learned that the ambassador did go down and investigate the schooner and the drums personally, and when he saw them—all they ever had in them was water—he realized that what I had told him about

183

the drums was irrefutably true. And he said, "This is terrible. It was all a lie—everything they charged these men with was a lie."

They sent me back on the *Santa Rosa* to New York. For me it was the end of something; I knew I never wanted again to be mixed up in those things. Something totally different had to begin.

I thought I would make a goddam fortune. But I made nothing. And I really knew I was going to make nothing. This trip was a total loss. Simpson took his share and mine, too, after we got out of jail. Honest John later got his share, but Simpson walked off with mine and married a girl fifty years his junior and squandered it all on her.

The truth was, I was really running away from myself, from becoming civilized.

And running from a girl I had met indirectly through Hank Hemingway—this girl Sandy, whom I realized I was crazy in love with and really wanted to marry.


Years later, during World War II, I came to Havana from New York. We ran alone, dodging submarines, and when we finally got safely into Havana Harbor, I heaved a big, bastardly sigh of relief and headed for the Uncle Sam Bar, the headquarters of most Caribbean pirates.

Sitting at one of the marble-topped tables, guzzling a frosty daiquiri, was old Honest John.

"Jake!!" he said. "You're back! Sit down, son. How've you been? Talk to me; give me a few kind words."

When I told him I'd brought in a big freighter from New York, his eyes lit up like a Chinese whorehouse.

184

"That's great, Jake," he said; "now we can do business in a big way."

I said, "No, John, you damn pirate. There's a big son-of-a-bitch war on and I have no time for hanky-panky. We've got to win this war."

He was disappointed. Things had been dull, he said. Christ, what with war, destroyers, airplanes, patrols, and all that, an honest smuggler couldn't get off the ground.

"How about Simpson?" he asked. "You kill him yet?"

"Kill him? Why kill him?"

John shrugged his shoulders significantly. "He gouged you out of forty thousand dollars."

It seemed perfectly clear that Honest John thought Simpson should be dead.

I explained to him that I had reasoned it all out: Sure, he gypped me out of the forty thousand, but he had problems.

"What problems?" Honest John asked, stroking his goatee.

"He married a young hash slinger, right? And, for Chrissakes, he was old and not very damned pretty. I doubt if he could get it up more than once a month. So what can he hold this gal with—his charm, his beauty? He knew I would scrounge around, shake the trees, rattle the bushes, and make more dough, but he couldn't. He was finished. And he loved this gal and had to hold her."

John looked at me, shaking his head sadly. "Jake," he said, "your logic is screwball."

"Screwball or not, John," I said, "I had to figure it out this way. But I promise you—I would have killed him otherwise."

185

We had some more drinks; in fact, we got pretty goddam drunk and sailed the big three-masted schooner all over again in our alcoholic euphoria.

Of course, Simpson and Honest John also got sent back. But neither of them wanted any part of going back to New York. Honest John, speaking for both of them, said to the embassy man, "Send us back to Havana."

That was home for them.

## 24. Simpson's Diamonds

*One of the things I heard Stein tell Arnold several times, in assorted ways, was that people and animals and fish and things had to be what they were, that they really couldn't change very much anyway. You had to accept them or reject them, but don't try to change them over.*

*But you had to know the difference between the real and false. The real essence and the real outside. Like a real diamond or a phoney diamond. A blue-white diamond or an industrial. Or a ten-cent-store diamond made of pure glass.*

*As it happened, I got myself snafued in all three varieties.*

This story of Simpson and the diamonds was part of that junket to South America.

We stopped at a lot of places en route with our cargo of "books" for the good sisters. We had two sets of sails—one good set we used out on the open sea; the other, a tattered, beat-up old set we used for going into port at the various

187

islands or along the coast of South America. We wanted to look shabby as hell so they wouldn't get suspicious about our carrying anything really valuable. One place we stopped at was British Guiana. In the jungles up the river, there were diamond fields. Industrial diamonds, but still worth a hell of a lot of dough—if you had enough.

Simpson got the idea of going up the river and getting some of those diamonds. We argued a lot about whether to do this or not on our voyage down. We argued about a hell of a lot of things on that trip. Sometimes you'd think it was life or death.

One time I remember, Simpson and I were in the cabin arguing about whether to go the shortest way, across the Gulf of Paria (between Trinidad and Venezuela), or the long way, on the outside. The short way was inside, through the Dragon's Mouth. The Serpent's Tooth was reached by the longer route, down Trinidad's eastern coast. So he and I were arguing in the cabin and Honest John was cooking. I looked up and there was Honest John standing at the stove trying to cook with his fingers crossed. "What the fuck are you doing, Honest John?" I asked.

He says, "Will you two stop talking—stop saying those things."

I asked him what things and he said, "Oh, what you're talking about."

I said, "What the hell are you talking about? You mean—the Serpent's Tooth?"

Very upset, he said, "Never mind, never mind. Please—just don't be using those words. Just let me get in here and cook."

Suddenly it came to me. Every time he heard one of

those words—serpent, or snake, or dragon—he had to cross his fingers.

You sure can't cook with your fingers crossed. It gave me a moment of thinking about people—what they are and aren't. Honest John—big-time hood, smuggler. He could mingle with all the cutthroats and killers across the world. But he was frightened and had to cross his fingers when he heard words like dragon or snake.

Maybe what Stein meant, telling Arnold that people are and have to be what they are, was that basically the differences are not that great anyway. Little or big, heroes or craven. All of us. For instance, I was afraid about going up that river in British Guiana with Simpson. It was a lonely and dangerous region—and you could never tell what might appear. Personally, I prefer the open sea. But we left in an outboard canoe, leaving Honest John to keep watch on the boat. It was just Simpson and me going up the river.

Way up the river, in the diamond fields, you get native diggers to do the work of scrubbing the earth, clawing the earth for diamonds. The diggers do the work and turn the stuff over to you.

The first night, we stayed in tents that we had to set up, waiting for the diggers to bring in our diamonds. When they finally showed up they had exactly two dingy diamonds. I said, "My God, is that all we're getting for this?"

Simpson, who was playing solitaire in the tent, didn't even bother to look up. The diggers went out. That was it; what could we do? So Simpson and I played cards in the goddam hot, stinky night. Then in comes a young native boy who was not one of our diggers at all. And this boy opens his belt and drops in front of us a real pile of diamonds. It was something just to look at them. Even if they were industrials, they were worth real dough—thirty to forty thousand at least.

Then we started bargaining with this native and finally got a deal. So when he left, after we made the deal, I said to Simpson, "How come—all that from a guy we never saw before?"

Simpson says, "Oh, he works for those two Dutchmen up the river a ways."

"You mean—he holds out from his people and sells to us?"

Simpson said, "That's it. It's part of the way they do business. It's quite all right. You see, our fellows right now are selling the Dutchmen the stones they're holding out on us."

British Guiana diamonds were a tricky business. You had to learn and follow the patterns—the way they were. On the way down the river, you put about 10 per cent of the diamonds in a little bag, and when you get down and turn in your gear the fellow at the British customs asks, "Well, how is it, old chap?"

"Oh—not much luck. Poor hunting. We did get a few."

You hold up the little bag with its approximately 10 per cent of what you really took. And you say to the man, "Come to think of it, this much really isn't worth worrying about. Why don't you take it?"

And you toss it and he catches it in the air, puts it in his pocket, and walks away.

We went away with our full load of diamonds in the other sack and no questions asked. The customs man goes off to the next hunter coming back with diggers and his diggings.

Not bad for a day's work. Things are what they are, as Stein would say.

Of course, all the way down we were figuring the big amount of dough we made, but the truth was we got not one dime of it. Because later, when our schooner was seized and we got thrown into that murderous jail, they took everything on board the vessel, including that bag of diamonds we had obtained—legally—in those fields up the river in Dutch Guiana.

As a matter of fact, legal or not, you couldn't stay very long up in those fields, because you really couldn't sleep up there. You sleep in cat naps and worry all through that, because you could get rolled and probably killed. They bury the bodies right there; they don't let them go floating down the river—that way there might be some clues left. And finding anybody's grave in that jungle is a lost cause. You just disappear, and that's the end of that.


When I finally got back to New York, there were no diamonds to spill into Sandy's hands.

But there was trouble. Sandy was in the hospital. Nobody knew, at the time, what was wrong, but whatever it was, her mother blamed it on me and told me in no mincing terms I had to stay away from her daughter forever. "Don't you ever see her again," she told me. "If you try to come anywhere near her, I'll have the law on you."

I'd made one bad mistake with Sandy's mother. One warm Saturday, when I'd been at Sandy's home, I inadvertently took off my suit jacket and her mother happened to glimpse the two shoulder-holster guns I always wore for self-protection during that time of my life.

191

I think that was when she began to feel twinges of concern about her daughter marrying me.

I found out through some of Sandy's friends that she was in a hospital over on Eighteenth Street and I went over and asked to see her, and the receptionist said, "Are you Mr. Klimo?"

I said yes. She said, "I'm sorry. I have orders you are not supposed to see her."

"Listen, honey," I told her very quietly, "I'm going to give warning. You had better go call some guards. Because I am going to see her."

The receptionist said, "Now, wait a minute, wait a minute."

I said, "You might as well go call the cops because I am going right through this hospital and find that girl. And anybody who tries to stop me can go shit in his hat."

She looked really shook up at that and asked, "Please—what is this all about?"

"Listen. It's real simple. We're in love. I'm going to marry her. But her mother doesn't want this marriage to happen. She's doing her damnedest to keep us apart. Now, where the hell is Sandy?"

The girl seemed to be softening a little as I spread new light on the problem. She finally said, "I'll give you the number if you promise not to tell anyone I gave it to you."

She gave me the number and I shot up there and discovered Sandy was just coming out of the anaesthetic. She had had an appendectomy and she was all right. Everything was fine. Unfortunately, just then Sandy's mother came in. She'd had word from the hospital that I was there. Right there in the sickroom she began angrily ordering me out and threatening me with arrest. I said, "Wait a minute, wait a minute. Not in here, the girl needs rest and peace. Come on outside. Come out in the hall."

Outside I changed my approach. I said, "Now, listen, lady. You're about sixty years old or more. I don't know how old you are. I don't care. But if you ever try to get between me and that girl again like you did just now, I'm going to bust you right between your baby blue eyes."

She looked pale, but she said, with great dignity and calm, "You wouldn't dare."

I told her just to try me. "I don't care if you are a little old lady, I'll bust you right between the horns. Now get out of my way, because I'm going in to Sandy."

After that, I was able to see Sandy without any argument, even after she returned to her mother's apartment. But the tensions were growing, and finally I said to Sandy, "Look, let's resolve the whole goddam thing. I've been seeing you for months and months and your mother's going nuts. I can cut her out of the whole thing by marrying you. How about it?"

For a moment, Sandy looked out the window. I didn't know what the hell she was thinking. I never asked. But she must have been thinking about it, because she said, "All right. We might as well."

I said, "Okay. We're getting married. I'll set the thing up."

And I go roaring out of there. I'm going to set the thing up. We'd already been talking about this for some time and we had our license, our blood tests, and all that crap, and now it's Saturday morning and it's all set except I have to find someone to marry us.

193

I hadn't yet figured out that part. I walked a ways and there were two cops talking and jabbering and telling each other how good they are. Two big, fat-bellied bastards. I came roaring up to them and said, "Hey, where's the justice of the peace?"

They stopped jabbering and looked at me. One asked me, "What do you want a justice of the peace for?"

I was still fresh out of that South American jail and I was leery of anything in uniform. I said, "Well, I want to get married."

Well, these two Irish cops really reacted. "Now, don't go off half cocked," they told me. "It's none of our business, but why don't you get married in a church?"

Anyway, they pointed out, there are no justices of the peace available in the city of New York on Saturdays. The magistrates' courts are closed on Saturdays.

"What else is available?"

"Marry her in a church. That's available."

They pointed down the street and there's St. Bartholomew's, on Park Avenue, one of the biggest, swankiest Protestant Episcopal churches there is. I open the door and, of course, it's Saturday and it's all silent and dead shadowy. But I can hear some voices behind the altar and I go back and there's a man in a turned-around collar and he wants to know what I want and I said, "Well, I want to get married."

He said, "Oh, fine. Now, what denomination are you?"

I said, "I'm nothing."

"You have never been baptized?"

"No. Never, and I don't belong to any church."

"Well, then, I really can't marry you."

194

"What do you have to do to get me married?" I asked.

"First I have to baptize you. That's an absolute essential."

I said, "Okay. Baptize me. Sprinkle the water. Say the words, whatever it is. I'm perfectly willing to go through whatever it has to be."

"No, no," he says. "First of all—about the young lady you want to marry. What religion is she?"

"I think she's an Episcopalian."

"Oh, good. I'm going to give you two little books I want both of you to read carefully. Then you come back in a few days and we'll talk."

Come back and talk! I told him I *had* to get married. Soon. Like today.

Not possible, he said. Not possible that way at all. I said the hell with it. I went out of the church and walked over to Lexington Avenue, where I saw a place called the White Rose Irish Bar. I went in to get a drink and talk the problem out with the bartender.

I'm telling him the whole bit and suddenly he breaks in and says, "Look, mister. You want to get married? Then, get a justice of the peace. That's all."

I said, "Right. But there aren't any available in New York. Not on Saturday."

He said, "Sure, that's right. But that's in New York City. There are some available in Yonkers. They're open any time, day or night."

I thanked him for that wonderful bit of information. I left him a dollar tip and got out a Yonkers directory. There I found the name of one Santo Caruso, J.P. I got him on the phone and I said, "Can you get me married without any hoo-rah?"

And he says, "You can get married without anything at all as long as you have the necessary documents and my fee."

"I've got the certificate and the marriage license. Everything. I want to get married. I just don't want any goddam barbaric ritual."

He says to me, "Sure, I'll do it. Now, you take the Broadway subway and you go to the end of the line, go downstairs, and wait there outside the park. I'll pick you up."

I said, "How will you know me?"

He said, "I'll know you, all right. I'll be driving a gray Plymouth two-door and smoking a cigar."

On the way up I picked up a friend of mine, Peter Vest, an old buddy I met in the theater, who worked as make-up artist at Elizabeth Arden's place on Fifth Avenue. I went steaming through this fruity place till I found him on the third floor, explained I needed him for a witness, and practically dragged him out. As we reached the street he asked me, "You got the ring?"

I didn't. I said, "Jesus Christ, no. But you wait right here. I'll be back in five minutes."

We were standing outside a five-and-ten. I went in and found they had wedding rings at ten and fifteen cents. There was nothing cheap about me; I bought the fifteen-cent ring and rejoined Peter on the street, the neatly wrapped package in my pocket.

We picked up Sandy and took the subway to the Bronx, where we got off and waited by the park. After a few minutes an old, beat-up Plymouth came careening around the park and a guy stuck his head out the window as he shot

196

past and yelled. "Are you Klimo?" I yelled back, "Yeah. Are you Caruso?" The cigar bobbed up and down, and the Plymouth clanked to a halt. We got in—Sandy, Peter, and I.

The J.P. wanted to know what price ceremony we wanted. I told him the cheapest he had available because we were hellishly short of cash.

We had the ceremony right there in his office. It was so cheap the J.P. didn't even bother to put out his cigar. He just placed it in a big glass ash tray on the side of his desk, went through the ritual at full speed ahead, and when it was all done, he pronounced us man and wife, picked up his smoldering cigar, and went on smoking. He'd scarcely missed a puff.

For Sandy and me it didn't matter. We were married, and all the furies of hell and her mother couldn't stop us. When my best man handed me that little box I'd bought earlier, with the ring in it, and I placed the ring on her hand with those words, "With this ring I thee wed and do herewith pledge my troth"—or words to that effect—it was the most significant moment in my life.

That ring I put on her finger is to this day a very precious symbol. They weren't real diamonds. They weren't even industrial diamonds from the fields in British Guiana. It was strictly a ten-cent-store ring—fresh that morning out of Woolworth's.

But, god damn—for us it glittered like real.

## 25.   End of a Revolution

Sometimes, at the big parties Stein and his pals were part of in those early days when Hank and I were living in Havana Harbor on the 18-footer, I'd hear Stein say things that sounded like absolute madness. Later I came to realize they were something quite different.

I remember at one of those parties somebody asked him, "Are you going back to Africa to hunt lions again?"

Stein's answer came back swiftly, almost as if he had a thing all ready in his mind, "No, not to Africa and not to hunt animals. I'm going to Spain and I'm going to be hunting tanks. They make bigger tracks."

I was startled by this, because it made no sense to me. In those early years of the thirties, Spain was not involved in any civil war, nor was there any such bloodletting business on the horizon.

This was two or more years before the Franco rebellion began. How did Stein know that far ahead so explicitly and accurately about that war and those tanks that he would be writing about and probing so brilliantly in *For Whom the Bell Tolls*?

Years after that remark he made about hunting tanks in Spain, I was in New York City and I ran into friends who knew that at that moment I was low in funds, having just quit the acting job I'd had in Milford, Connecticut. One of these friends suggested, "Jake, Hemingway's play, *The Fifth Column*, is about to go into production—they're having casting calls. You know Hemingway. Why don't you go get yourself a job?"

I knew Stein was there and I knew they were casting. But I had a deep feeling about this. I wouldn't use pull or presume on friendship, especially not with a man like Stein. I wasn't about to walk in and put him on the spot that way. And I knew damn well that if nobody else respected or understood my reasons, Stein would.

Sometime after that I ran into Hank Hemingway in New York. This was in the late thirties and I'd been sailing intermittently on freighters for some time during this period.

Hank seemed glad to see me and wanted to know where I'd been all these months.

"I just got back from working on a freighter that took me around the world," I said.

"Did you stop off in Spain?"

"No. Why?"

"My God, Jake," he said. "Don't you realize the hell going on over there? Haven't you read the stories of what's happening?"

I saw he was really hot about this thing and I said, "Look,

199

I've heard and read a hell of a lot of stuff about it. But you know it's hard to tell from the stories. A lot of it may be plain bullshit. Written from the wrong side."

Hank admitted that was probably true, and I said, "Hank, you tell me. You're in this apparently up to your asshole. What does Stein say about it?"

"Oh, Stein says this is it. This is the thing; this is the real fight. Right there, right now." Then he looked at me oddly and said, "You're not going?"

"You think I should?"

"You're damned right about that. I think you owe it to yourself and even to Stein. This is something he believes in, too."

I didn't quite understand what Hank was getting at except maybe Hank thought that now I needed direction for myself, my future. I said, "Well, look, this idea is all new to me. Let me think it over. I'll talk to you in a couple of days."

We met a few times more and talked about the growing peril of fascism if it were finally to take over in Spain the way it had in Hitler's Germany. These were issues deep in our conscience and consciousness at that period in our own lives.

Finally, about a week later, I said to him, "Hank, you've been blowing up this storm about Spain and my going over there because Stein's over there and they need volunteers to fight Franco and Hitler. What about you? How about the two of us joining the Lincoln Brigade and going over together?"

Hank said no, he wasn't volunteering for this war. He said anybody who could go should go. But he had other obligations, where I didn't. He wasn't just thinking about himself; he had to think also about his wife and offspring. "I've got to make a living; I've got to take care of them. They are my first responsibility."

I couldn't deny the validity of what he said. I said, "I understand, Hank. But why are you so hot for getting me over there?"

"Because you've only yourself to take care of, Jake. And they need guys like you—there."

I realized that Hank did feel his responsibilities, the bonds of his obligations. But he still wanted to go to Spain, because Stein was there and the war was there.

I told him that in so many words. I said, "Hank, you really want me to go, partly anyway, because that way you can be there vicariously. Because you really do want to go and feel you can't. And that's one reason why you want me to go."

He said nothing, but I knew from his expression that he could not deny what I said.

Then I added, "Hank, it doesn't matter what your reasons are. You've sold me. I'll go. Franco is a son-of-a-bitch. I'd like to get in there for the kill. I'll go if I can fly a plane," I said. "I'll go if I can fly for the Spanish Republic. But I won't crawl through the mud. How about them apples?"

"That's what they need most," he said. "Flyers."

"Okay. What do we do?"

"We have to go down and see Jay Allen. He's the guy in charge of running the underground—recruiting for the Spanish Republic. He's down at Washington Square, in the Village."

Jay Allen was the author of a number of political articles

201

and books that stirred up a storm in Washington, where he once worked for the State Department, exposing what went on behind the scenes of our own government.

Like many others of that era, he joined the forces of the political left in America, which at that time were totally supporting the Spanish Republican forces.

Allen told me I was just the kind of fighter and flyer they wanted, but the big question was—how did they get me over there? Government restrictions were tightening, and with Franco forces taking over more and more of Spain, it was becoming increasingly difficult to get volunteers into the struggle.

I told him I had heard that Bert Acosta, the famous aviator of that time, was going over there. Maybe I could go with him. I didn't explain that I'd run into Bert first when he was in the business of flying Chinamen into Florida via Havana.

Allen looked jolted when I asked about Acosta. "Don't you know what Bert is doing now?" he said. "He's not flying for the Spanish Republic. He's flying for Franco."

I said I could hardly believe Bert would do that. Allen insisted it was the truth. I was never able to verify it and don't know to this day that he actually did fly for Franco.

Allen said there were only two ways for me to get over. "You can go through Canada. That could take as long as two months. Maybe longer."

I told him it sounded like a hell of a long time to me. Jay said. "Well, it's too bad you're not a sailor. Then we could get you over on a hospital ship."

I said, "Look, god damn it, I *am* a sailor. I've been a

sailor as long as I can recall. I've got my AB ticket right here in my pocket."

"You're an able-bodied seaman in good standing?"

"Right. Right as all hell."

"Well, that does it. You can go on the hospital ship. No sweat at all. We'll sign you on as an AB. Then, when she gets to Spain, you jump ship. They'll have all the papers over there."

For once in my life I was doing something I felt was honest and totally unselfish. I was fighting for a cause, not for money. I suppose I did have a second reason—Stein himself. Because Hank had given me some of that information about what his brother was doing and where I'd find him.

And even though I understood Hank's own motivations, I also had a deep desire to see Stein again, to talk with him at this new level. This was a cause to which Stein had dedicated himself and, to some degree, his life. It was to produce one of his two or three greatest books, reflecting the soul of the Spanish people and the agony of a war that rubbed out any hope of freedom in Spain for decades to come.

With most of the young of that time, I felt that Stein was doing the finest thing of his life, and I wanted to tell him so, and to let him know I was there too. I would be there flying—risking and maybe even losing my life—for this cause.

One day later I was aboard the hospital ship as an able-bodied seaman, helping with the big hawsers as she backed out of the pier and into the stream and started down the harbor, heading out past the Statue of Liberty and Governors Island.

We were just about off Ambrose Light when suddenly all engines on the hospital ship stopped. I had no idea of what had happened. I began to realize that the vessel was swinging. She came full about, and a few minutes later was heading back up the harbor.

Word of what had happened finally trickled down as we headed to the pier we had just left. The Spanish Civil War was over. Generalissimo Franco was dictator of the whole Spanish people.

I could picture how Stein must have felt at that moment. He had been a driving force, a special kind of American hero to all Spaniards who defended the cause of the Spanish Loyalists.

Now it was over. The Republic was dead. Spain became a new stooge of Mussolini and Adolf Hitler, the captive of Franco and his military fascist government. That was how I and millions of other Americans saw it that day.

Almost a decade earlier, Stein had talked about the bigger tracks—the bigger meaning, the struggle for Spain. Now, with the battle lost, history itself could be taking a whole new turn. World War II lay just ahead.

The hospital ship nudged its way into its North River berth and we disembarked. My services were no longer needed.

But at least Stein would know I made the try.

# III

## Other Times, Other Wars

## 26. Men and Guns

*In the closing years of the 1930s I was riding not freight cars, as in my youth, but giant, twin-screw freighters all over the globe. Married or single, I still felt the sea was my mistress. Once the land fell away, I was safe. And I worked my way up in the echelons of the ships that sail the sea— eventually got to be third mate, and not too far beyond that I made first mate.*

*I went to almost every place you could think of or name, it seemed to me; all those strange, far-off places. A number of times in the States, I'd run into Stein, down in Florida especially.*

*We'd have a ball or two and talk. It was friendly, but not like the old times. He was older and grayer then; in those few but pleasant moments, I glimpsed a new Stein, for whom I was sure in my heart other bells had begun to toll.*

*It isn't easy to get a man like Stein out of your spleen;*

*the personality is too strong, there are too many facets. Like his books and stories, he himself reached out to your life in varying ways.*

During World War II we were held up for repairs in Beira, Portuguese East Africa, for about three weeks. Along about the third day, I was ashore, heading for the nearest bar, when I walked by a vacant lot. It was full of big, white, bleaching elephant skulls scattered around like tombstones.

I walked among them, thinking about Stein. Christ, here I was in Africa! I hadn't thought much about hunting. I had just been hunted by a submarine and was on the wrong end of the game.

In the bar I asked the bartender about going hunting.

"Not a chance," he said. "This isn't like the British colonies. You can't buy a license to hunt—only a Portuguese can hunt. We don't even let the natives hunt."

I said, "Got it pretty cozy, haven't you?" and walked out.

I was strolling up the road, kicking stones and cursing the Portuguese, when I heard a call behind me. When I turned, I saw a man waving at me. A fine-looking man, big, tanned, and well muscled, with clear blue eyes and a wonderful, wide smile.

"I am Magalhães," he said, shaking my hand.

"That's Magellan," I said.

He nodded, pleased that I had recognized his name in Portuguese.

"I was in the bar," he said. "I heard you inquire about hunting."

I nodded.

"I am a contractor," he continued. "I build houses, bridges, whatever. Also, I like to hunt. In fact, I'd rather hunt than build. My wife says I waste all my time hunting. You know women." He shifted his feet and hesitated, embarrassed.

"I . . . I don't know how to say this," he began. "You want to hunt—I like to hunt and I also need lumber for my business. You need a safari—I need lumber." He smiled a big, winning smile, shrugged his shoulders, and spread his hands. "You have dunnage on your ship; this is the lumber I need. So we trade. I give you a safari and you give me dunnage."

We made the deal on the spot, and he insisted I come to his home for a drink. I met his wife—a delightful, beautiful woman who regarded me with suspicion and a slight distaste. I was going to steal her man off into the jungles.

"I must show you my house," Magalhães said, leading me to the basement, where six black servants were polishing silver. As we came down the stairs, they froze in their positions and stared at us—not a movement. Magalhães walked over to a long table with a big box at one end. As he moved toward it, I heard a soft pattering sound and turned to see what it was. Not a single servant remained; they had vanished up the stairs.

"This is my—I think you call it gymnasium," Magalhães said, patting the table. "In this box is a python."

"A what?" I hoped I hadn't heard what he had said.

"A snake; I will wrestle him." He stripped to the waist and placed his left hand by the door of the box.

"Open the top and stir him with the stick," Magalhães said, not taking his eyes off the door at the bottom of the

209

box. I jabbed with the stick, and a big head shot out the door. Magalhães grabbed the snake just behind the head and sidestepped with him as the long body slithered out on the table. The snake's tail began flicking about, searching for a hold. With his other hand, Magalhães kept prying the tail loose whenever it started to wrap around anything. His other hand was fighting the head, holding it away from his own body. His arms were never still—straining against the arching of the snake's head and fighting the flicking tail.

"I cannot let him anchor his tail," he gasped, straining and sweating, "or he will crush me."

I stepped back, suddenly realizing why the servants had taken to the hills. I was thinking of joining them.

The man and the snake strained and writhed for what seemed to be hours. It was actually only about ten minutes, and then the snake urinated—a great stream, covering one end of the table—and went limp.

Magalhães dropped the head and wiped his forehead with the back of his hand.

"God almighty, don't let that thing go!" I shouted.

Magalhães smiled. "No, Jake," he said. "He pissed. He is finished." He lifted the snake's head and let it drop. It plunked on the table like a wet dishrag. No fight left in the bastard at all.

"Come, we will stuff him back in the box," Magalhães said.

"*You* will stuff him back in the box," I said, keeping my distance.

Magalhães laughed. "You know, Jake, each day the

210

snake grows bigger and I grow older and weaker. Perhaps some day . . ."

"You're crazy," I said. "The snake's bound to win, sooner or later."

Magalhães shrugged. "Perhaps," he said. "But not to-day."

We left the next day in a Land-Rover and a truck filled with supplies. We followed the Ureme River, heading inland about 100 miles. It was quite a trip, especially after we left the roads. We crossed the Ureme on two longboats lashed together. After that, it was open savannah. Within three days we arrived at Magalhães' camp. We hunted during the day, getting reed buck, antelope, and gazelle, but we were really after lion. The third day, we saw a herd of antelope grazing between clumps of bushes. "We need meat," Magalhães said, and stopped the Land-Rover.

We took .22-caliber rifles and began stalking the animals, walking slowly, stopping now and then, making the same motions as grazing animals. Since we were down wind, the antelope couldn't smell us, and of course we never talked—the way they do, for instance, in the movies.

I was about to shoot when the gunbearer touched my arm and pointed. On the other side of a bush was the biggest damned lion I had ever seen. He had been stalking the same herd, and as we rounded the bush, we became aware of each other. He was staring at us, and then, Holy Christ, up comes another lion, and the two of them stare at us. Magalhães patted his .22, shook his head and motioned back to the Land-Rover. We backed carefully and slowly to the car, held up the guns, and the bearers swapped our .22's for the big-caliber rifles. Now we crept back toward

211

the lions, picking our way carefully, never taking our eyes off them.

When we got within range, Magalhães pointed to the one on the left and tapped his chest. That was his. Mine was to be the one on the right. We got set and Magalhães whistled. That was the signal to fire. When we fired, both lions leaped high and spooked out, running fast away from us. I shot the bolt of my rifle and was taking aim for the second time when I heard a thumping sound behind me. I turned and saw Magalhães stomping the butt of his rifle on the ground.

"Damned thing jammed," he said. I felt a strange, crawling feeling up the back of my neck. I hadn't been much worried before. I figured I had Magalhães to back me up. What if those lions had charged? One gun and two ball-busting lions coming at me!

"Yours is wounded," Magalhães told me. "Mine isn't. Goddam bad ammunition; no wonder my gun jammed." He pointed to a great swatch of elephant grass. "He's in there," he said. "Wait a while. If he doesn't come out, we go in and get him."

I stared at the gently waving grass and said to myself, "I don't want to go in there." It was as if I had said it aloud.

"Look, Jake," Magalhães said, "he's wounded and will charge anything that comes near. It could be a native—anybody. Also, he is in pain."

We waited about a half hour and then started in, moving very slowly, one step at a time. I came to a spot where the grass had thinned out, and was starting across the clearing, when I saw the tall grass shake slightly on the other side. I stopped and stared hard at the wall of elephant grass. It

212

parted and I saw the lion's head. I started firing, working the bolt as fast as I could, but that damned lion kept coming. He was roaring, clawing the ground, trying to reach me before my bullets reached him. He was four feet away, still howling and straining to get at me.

I had just emptied my gun when he stopped and fell.

Magalhães called for his gunbearer, who handed him a .22 rifle. He shot the lion in the shoulder. Its body didn't move. I was shaking and sweating, but this action puzzled me.

"Never trust a lion," Magalhães said. "Many men have been killed by rushing up to examine their kill. This way, we are certain he is dead."

Three days later we were sitting in camp drinking Portuguese brandy. It was night. We had hunted all day and were having a few drinks before turning in. A native padded up to Magalhães and murmured something. Magalhães set his drink down. He jabbered at the man. The other natives became agitated. What had been a sleepy camp turned into a throng of vibrating natives.

"There's a herd of Cape buffalo down by the river," Magalhães told me. "They want us to get one for them."

I remembered Stein's Cape buffalo and how the goddamned thing had trailed him, and what a huge, murderous creature it was. And these crazy natives wanted us to go out *at night* and get one!

Magalhães said, "Cape buffalo are always dangerous."

"It's crazy," I said. "To hell with it."

"No," Magalhães said. "These people are hungry. They can't kill a buffalo. They are not allowed guns."

We rigged our flashlights like miners' headlamps but without turning them on and started single file down the trail to the river. It was black as hell and the jungle noises were all around us—the god-damnedest yawping, screaming, grunting, and clacking I'd ever heard.

As we approached the river we slowed down until we were barely moving. Magalhães was the lead man, with me behind him. Suddenly he stopped and reached back, squeezing my arm, then pointed to the right. I strained my eyes and saw black shapes close by. It was the buffalo. Magalhães stepped off the trail and pulled me toward him, motioning me to ready my gun. We stood side by side, adjusting our lamps and checking the safeties on our guns. Magalhães did the same thing he had done with the lions—pointed to one dark blob, indicating it was mine, and to another, his.

Magalhães whistled. We switched on our lights and readied our guns. Jesus Christ! Those buffalo seemed to leap right toward us. I hadn't realized how close we were. They raised their heads high, pointing into the light. We both fired, and, Holy God! the whole world seemed to explode. The herd turned and stampeded, literally shaking the earth as they thundered away. Magalhães said something over his shoulder, and two trackers disappeared into the darkness. We stood perfectly still, guns cocked and at our shoulders. The trackers came back in a minute and spoke to Magalhães.

"They are wounded," he said, not taking his gun from his shoulder. "There is blood."

It came to me in a flash. Here I am, standing by an African river, in what had to be the blackest night this side of

214

hell, and we have wounded a Cape buffalo, the meanest, most dangerous animal in Africa, and now we are sitting ducks. I remembered Stein describing that buffalo trailing him through the elephant grass. How could Magalhães have gotten us into this spot? Then I realized it was his responsibility. These natives were hungry, not just a little bit hungry—there was a famine at that time. And Magalhães, as a Portuguese, was obligated to feed them. This was the first herd of buffalo in two months, and they might not come again. We stood stock-still, not moving an inch—listening, straining for the slightest sound. We remained that way for nearly an hour. These people were used to this; I wasn't. It was a terrible strain. Even when we started back, it seemed to take hours before we reached camp, stopping every few paces, freezing and listening.

During the rest of the safari, Magalhães kept sentinels stationed around the camp day and night.

"You never know," he explained. "That buffalo could show up anytime."

When I got back to the ship I threw a big party celebrating the hunt and invited Magalhães and his family. During the dinner, in the ship's saloon, all hell broke loose. The ship's wiper, a big oaf of a man, had been feuding with the third mate and they chose this time to settle their differences. The little third mate came scurrying right through the saloon with the big wiper thundering after him. I didn't care much if they killed each other, but, god damn it, they could do it out on deck or on the dock. They didn't have to break up the whole damn party.

The wiper was in a rage. As they circled the saloon I tripped him and he fell on his face. I jumped on him

215

and caught him in a headlock, bending his head forward on his chest. Suddenly, all the fight went out of him. I felt a tap on my shoulder. It was Magalhães. "Don't break his neck," he said gently. "He pissed."

I got up, and the wiper limped damply out of the saloon.

The only hunting I have done since was for pheasants out in Iowa, and I like pheasants . . . they taste goddam good. I remember cleaning pheasants once and one of the hunters saying, "Hell, Jake, this must be tame stuff to you after lion and buffalo."

I thought about that for a while, and said, "No, you're wrong. I'm hunting now for food. I'll never hunt big game again in my life. Fact is, they should pass an international law—no, make it stronger. Something like the Golden Rule. Make it say, 'A man must eat whatever he shoots.'"

People were getting pretty used to sudden violent death in those goddam times. Especially as stories of Hitler's concentration camps and their brutalities and killing began to leak out, even then.

Once in New York City—this was well before I married Sandy—Hank came to me with a story about how submarines—Nazi "killer" subs—were prowling off the waters of South America. I said, "Hell, Hank, they've been doing that for the last three years. Everybody down there knows about it. Our intelligence knows about it. How can they help but know?"

Hank said he wasn't too sure our intelligence people knew very much, certainly not as much as they should know. In any case, why didn't we get a schooner and or-

216

ganize our own hunting party? Go out and get the story of those German submarines?

"You know where they are, Jake?"

I said, "You're damn right I know. Plenty of nights on the schooner I sat there in the dark and I could hear those bastards. I could hear them talking. They were that close."

We could hear their engines, I told him. We could sit in the dark and hear the throbbing underneath us. Because we didn't have an engine, we ran with sails—nothing else. Didn't even carry a radio.

I said I wasn't going with him on any cruise anywhere right at that time. I said I'd decided once and for all to marry Sandy. Hank said something about how I should be pretty sure before I made the big step.

The truth was, Hank Hemingway and my mother had sort of ganged up on me; they wanted me to marry a girl they'd picked out for me—one of the local Iowa varieties that I wanted no part of.

I was sore about it for a time, and I really hit the overhead when he started in about it again at this late date. It was just one of those human things that happen, I suppose. On his side and mine as well.

Anyway, Hank did organize a cruise and got a schooner and a couple of other fellows and they went down to the Caribbean off South America and came up with a pretty sharp yarn called "Snoop Cruise," which was published by *Reader's Digest*.

The story did make our Navy intelligence look not very bright, as though they didn't know what was happening, which I really suspect was not the case. I think they had the whole business ticketed but kept that fact well covered.

217

There were no Pearl Harbors on the East Coast—or off South America.

The Navy people naturally were sore as hell about that piece and told Hank so when he went down a few months later to apply for a Navy commission after America got into the war. They said in effect, "You're the so-and-so who wrote that *Reader's Digest* story about how dumb the Navy is."

Hank joined the Army.

Hank was pretty close to my mother for quite a while; he got to know her because his wife, Patsy, was out there for some time staying with my parents while she was pregnant the second time. We see ourselves and we see others in different ways; we don't always understand how right we can be—and how wrong—even about our own parents and relatives. Both Hank and I had had to make adjustments.

I got to understand after a while how much my father drove himself at his job. It was all he had. Mother wanted to travel, travel, travel, and he wanted to stay peacefully put in one place, with all his sons around. That would have been his fulfillment, and it couldn't ever happen and never did.

There used to be a clothes chute in our house that I would open at night sometimes and listen to my mother and father arguing. I remember once hearing him say to her, "You've driven all my sons away. I've got nothing."

I realized ultimately how sedentary and set in his ways he was. But I loved him; I really loved my father. I did badger him, though, as a youth. I was smart, pretty fresh. I remember once when I came back during this later period and we got talking, really down to the core of things, and I said, because of something he was sort of boasting about, "Tell me, Pop—are you very proud of the fact that you've slept only with my mother and no other woman?"

He thought about that for a moment and said, "Well, yeah, I guess I am."

I said, "Well, Jesus Christ, I don't think that's anything to be proud of."

He didn't say anything. He just looked at me and shook his head.

But he had his sense of humor. He was sitting there one day watching television—this was a long time later. And I said, "My God, Pappy, how can you sit and watch a damn ball game all afternoon?"

He said, "Don't you think watching a ball game is fun?"

I said, "Pappy, with the little time I've got to myself, I'm not going to spend it watching a bunch of grown men hitting a ball around the field. I'm going to get a big bottle and a big blonde and go to bed."

And he just laughed till tears ran down his face and he couldn't see the damn ball game.

I get talking about my father and I remember things. I recall when I was fifteen years old and he was reading the newspaper and I said, "Hey, Pappy, I think I'll go to Mexico."

He looked from his paper and he said, "When are you leaving?"

I said, "Tomorrow morning."

And he said, "Okay." And went back to the paper. He was aging even then and he was semiparalyzed.

I quit going to sea for a time years later, and Sandy and I went out there to take care of my father, now a widower, in Mount Vernon. We stayed nearly five years.

Those last years were quite a trying time. I went broke out there, and took a lot of crazy jobs. I wound up, for example, in Mount Vernon being what they called a "turd wrassler"—a sewer-pipe layer in the main street of the town. I was also a machinist for two years, a cement foreman on a big flood-control dam project, a bartender, and a wine maker.

My father died in the midfifties, and Sandy and I left almost right away. I didn't want to stay out there; the only reason I'd been there was because of him. We went back East and I got myself a job building a wing onto a man's house on Long Island. I'd never held a hammer seriously before, but I did a beautiful job on that addition, put the sewer piping in, poured the concrete, did the whole thing —it took a year.

Then that job ran out and I got a job skippering a 50-foot motor yacht out of Freeport, Long Island. I had my master's license by then and got the job by putting an ad in the paper: "Master mariner wants job skippering yacht."

The owner turns out to be a man about seventy-four. He points to this 50-footer tied up at the dock in the Freeport canal and he asks me, "Know anything about that boat?"

I said no.

"Handled one like it?"

"No."

"Then, why in hell are you applying for a job like this?"

I told him I'd run all kinds of ships and boats all over

the world. I said, "I've docked a big, three-masted schooner without any engines at all, luffed her up to a dock no bigger than yours, gentle as a baby in a crib." I said, "I think I can handle your yacht."

Well, he said, he didn't have time to waste. We'd take her out at once. If I could handle her, I was hired.

So I went on board and started the engines up. I felt the throttles. I surged her forward and surged her back with the lines still fast to the pilings. Then I cast off the lines, brought her out into the channel, and using only the gears of the two engines, without touching the wheel or the throttle, I turned her around 180 degrees, then brought her full around, backed her into the dock, and tied up. All this while he stood watching. After I made the lines fast, he said, "You're a liar. You've handled boats like this before."

I told him I was no liar and I resented his saying that. I said I was a real sailor and I could handle any goddam thing on the sea.

So he said I had the job. I took it, because I needed every cent of money to feed my family. I got a job part time in addition working on the docks in Greenpoint, Brooklyn, but he found out about that and told me I had to quit that job.

I said "Why?"

"Because I'm paying you and I don't want you working for anybody else on your days off. Nobody else, understood?"

I tried to explain to him that I needed the extra money for my family, but he just brushed that aside. I work for him and nobody else—days off or not. I was outraged. I

221

said, "You're paying me a fucking hundred a week and you figure I'm your goddam slavey?" I couldn't believe what I was hearing. I said, "Mister, you don't understand. I won't work for you. Because you're a prick. And I don't work for pricks."

He stood staring at me as if he couldn't grasp what I was saying, as if he couldn't accept the fact that I was human, like him. That I had needs and a family to feed. He couldn't stand the idea that he was paying me but I was still free enough to work for somebody else in my free time.

Unlike his boat, I was not his exclusive personal property, bought and paid for and subject to his whims.

I said very little more. I handed him the keys and went below to get my gear. As I came off the yacht, he began to think twice, and he offered me a small increase in wages. I said, "I'm sorry, but you're a prick, and I wouldn't ever go on working for a prick."

And I walked up that street without ever looking back.

## 27.  A Government Call

It beats all hell, the way I see it, how things get turned around in life. Like one thing that happened between Hank and me.

This began about the time the war broke out in Europe. Right about then I was trying to get somewhere in the theater. The boys in Havana were still hollering for me to come down and get back into the swing of things, but I was buying no more of that. It was over forever. I had Sandy, and that was more important. I used to tell her, "Jesus Christ, here I am shuffling around for peanuts as a ham actor. What am I doing it for? I should be doing something more lucrative."

And Sandy would look worried that it might be something she didn't approve of. And I would say, "Don't worry, Sandy, that's all dead and gone." But I did know I was no good as a fucking ham actor. Acting just wasn't in my blood—not the way the sea is in my blood. The stage is a

223

tinselly thing, full of hysterical nuts. There were some good people in it, some very good people, but it's not real, it just isn't real.

Anyway, Sandy was working and supporting the two of us and I couldn't stand that, and I went down to the waterfront to sniff around, ran into some old shipmates, and began hearing about a new training station out in the harbor, where they were training up merchant-marine people.

I said, "The hell they are. What are they teaching?"

"Well, they're teaching you how to be a sailor, Jake. But you have to have been at sea three years."

I'd been to sea a hell of a lot more years than that. I'd sailed freighters and schooners just about all over the world. And now they were going to teach me how to be a sailor.

I thought it was pretty funny. But then I thought it would give me more time to be with Sandy, so I went out and joined up. And they taught me how to be a sailor. That really tickled the hell out of me.

Of course, I couldn't see Sandy at all—for the duration of the training period everybody was quarantined. No visitors.

But some of those instructors in that thing realized pretty quick that I was a sailor—and a canvas sailor at that. One of the top men in the program said to me, "You want to stick around and be a teacher?"

I said "Sure, fine. What would I teach?" And they said, "You'll teach these young guys to be sailors. There's a war on. We may find ourselves in the middle of it, too."

I stayed and taught. Soon we were building Liberty ships, and Sheepshead Bay, off New York Harbor, turned into a real shipping center for the war. The thing boomed and boomed, with thousands of young guys coming into the program for training. I wound up as assistant training officer. I was fourth in command for the whole shebang. There was the superintendent, the exec officer, the training officer, and I.

Mainly, what I was teaching was not navigation as much as seamanship, training these young bucks for sea duty in the war. I stayed out there training these men for two and a half years. Then I got the patriotic urge—I didn't want to stay inside teaching. I had to go out there myself.

I really had itchy feet, but I told Sandy I didn't want to go as an enlisted man. I wanted to go to war but not before the mast—not jammed up there in the fo'c'sle. I said, "Look, I've skippered my own schooners. I'm a better sailor than any son-of-a-bitch a steamship can turn out."

I said, "I'm not going back as a crew member. And I'm not much interested in skippering the goddam things. But I do want my own room. I want privacy. I want quiet. I want my own bed and comfort, and a record player to play my own music; I want a typewriter to type and good books to read, and until they torpedo me, I want to be able to sit back in comfort and enjoy these simple pleasures."

Anyway, I went up to New London and took the courses and learned celestial navigation all over again and came out an officer and ultimately passed the exam for my master's license. That really surprised Sandy, because I'd told her over and over how I flunked the multiplication tables in third grade and never got beyond that point in mathematics.

I never gave up being uncivilized, of course—but I was civilized enough to be an officer. Once, there was a big ammunition explosion in Bombay, and when we came in with a full cargo load on our ship, the harbor master said we'd be there three months or longer unloading because of the damage to the port.

As chief mate, I told my good friend the skipper that something had to be done about the crew's sex problem; there was a shortage of whores in Bombay and VD was rampant. I told the old man, "Let's play it smart. These men are going up there and pick up real trouble if we don't do something. There are thousands of sailors in this port right now in the same situation."

I outlined my plan. "Let's pool all the funds available and go up there and take one of the houses. Just for our crew, nobody else. Buy it for the duration, girls included.

The old man said it was a brilliant inspiration. He told me to go in there and set it up.

Well, I went in and shopped around, asked a lot of questions, and finally wound up in a place way up on a hill —an out-of-the-way little house with only four girls. This was Susie's Place. Susie was a hard-boiled business woman, and we had a lengthy discussion about financing this unorthodox setup. She finally agreed to a three-month plan— the ship would put up funds for the house and girls for the whole period. Nobody else gets in. The men worked out the schedule so everybody had a regular turn of duty on the ship and in the whorehouse.

I insisted all the girls go with me to the company doctor for examination. When we arrived I sent word inside to the doctor, "I've got four able-bodied seamen here for you to check on."

And I sent in the four girls all at once in their pretty

Indian saris. When he saw the "seamen," he started laughing. This was all highly irregular. But he gave them a good and thorough examination, which they passed with flying colors. All the men were examined, too—all but one made it.

Susie's Place remained the ship's exclusive property for the next three and a half months—until we pulled out of Bombay. The men kept up the schedules. There was never a single case of VD on board.

At the end of the first month there were only fifteen ships in the harbor; that doubled and quadrupled in the ensuing weeks. No one on board ever let on as to the whereabouts of Susie's little hideout. Only one sailor from another boat got into this private preserve, and he had to swear secrecy to me and take a medical test besides.

Rumors did spread fast in a harbor like that. Somehow, because of this well-organized project, the story spread all the way to America that I was the maharaja of all the party girls in the whole of Bombay. When I heard about this at the union hall after I got back, I was outraged. "My God," I demanded, "how could such a terrible story as that get started?"

Civilized or not, one real turnabout situation developed after I got back and had been named assistant training officer in the merchant marine seaman-training program. I was out at the training station in New York Harbor.

The phone rings on my desk. The fellow calling says he's the FBI. The Federal Bureau of Investigation. When he says this in that easy but official tone, I think: Oh, my God. They've really got me. Now they're going to lay in with all the past deeds of my whole mixed-up career. And I think, Holy Christ, they're finally catching up.

But the fellow talks very pleasant and says maybe I can be of some help to him, and he beats around the horse-feathers for a while and then he says, "By the way, do you know someone who calls himself Leicester Hemingway?"

Now, there was a switch. I said, "Yeah, yeah, sure I know him. What about him?"

"Well," the FBI man said, "he's applied for a post in the war effort and I want to ask you—would you be able to say that in your opinion, which the government holds very high, your friend Mr. Hemingway is a good security risk?"

Now I understood—they were putting on a security check regarding Hank Hemingway. I was being asked to vouch for his honesty and integrity, his probity, and similar matters.

I gave him the real build-up, naturally. I said, "Hemingway? You don't have to worry about him. He's 100 per cent. He loves his country, never joined the Commies or the Nazis, nothing like that at all."

"And you knew him pretty well?"

"Oh, yes. For a long time. Why, we were together on one stint on small boats for more than a year, a lot of the time on an 18-foot sloop. You get to know a man pretty well over a period like that, sailing in a small boat from one port to another in the Caribbean. Why, Mr. Hemingway even named his son after me. We've been good friends. I know he's a fine, loyal, trustworthy citizen. You don't have to worry about him. No, sir."

I meant all of this and it did apparently impress the FBI

man. "Well," he said, "coming from you in your position, this is certainly a fine report. We thank you very much."

From his tone I was sure Hank would have no trouble. Which, of course, he didn't.

But I hung up, shaking my head. There I was, an old reprobate with a checkered background that far back. And here I was vouching for the brother of Ernest Hemingway —for Hank Hemingway, who had never done anything wrong in his life, never even had a traffic ticket, as far as I knew.

And there was I—pirate and smuggler and all that, assuring the government that my friend never mingled with questionable characters.

And I sat there and laughed and laughed at such a goddam impossible thing.

229

## 28.  The Great Tomato-Paste Robbery

There came a day when the war-born shipping boom was over. A lot of our ships and lines were sold or transferred to foreign colors. Jobs were tight.

One day, in the Greenpoint waterfront area of Brooklyn, my stevedore pal Andy says, "Things are going to hell, Jake. I got no room for you on the docks. Unless you want to work in the hold. And you don't have the guts to do that."

I said, "What the hell makes you say that? I'll work in the hold."

He says, "I've seen you make those guys reload a couple of hatches when you were mate. They hate your guts."

"The hell they do," I said. "They didn't give a damn, because they worked by the hour. They're all my buddies."

"Bet you a case of whiskey," he says.

"Okay—the best you can buy."

"You got a bet, Jake. You show up here tomorrow morning, ready for work."

So I show up next morning with a hook. All the other guys are asking what the hell I'm doing there and wasn't I mate on the *Norwalk Victory* and wasn't I going to be skipper?

I said sure, but Black Diamond Line changed to a foreign flag and I have five kids to feed and I'm out of a job.

They put me on the gang and I went right down into the hold and muscled bales, loading and discharging and even driving forklifts on the dock. I carried on this work for eight months. And man—what a ball-busting job; but I stayed with it.

One night a very interesting thing happened. A complete bargeload of tomato paste vanished into thin air. A whole goddam barge. The next morning the empty barge was found beached on Staten Island.

Next thing I knew, I was called to the offices of Black Diamond, my former employers. They knew that I was working on the docks, and did I know anything about the operation?

The Black Diamond guy said, "Jake, you have any idea who was in on the job?"

"Are you out of your mind?" I demanded. "Are you sheer crazy? Don't you realize if I did know and I told you I'd be a floating corpse?"

"Well," he said, "We thought you might have seen something."

I said, "I don't know a damned thing. But now, since you called me in, I can't even go back to work on the docks

231

until this cools off. Somebody might get jumpy, figure I know something, and knock me off anyway."

I told him bluntly I didn't like it, I didn't like being called into the office.

"Well, Jake, I'm sorry," the Black Diamond official said. "What are you planning to do?"

"I'll try to get out to sea on something," I said, "a long, quiet ride somewhere, anywhere. Till the damn thing cools."

"Tell you what," he said. "I've heard that Isbrandtsen is trying to run that blockade Chiang Kai-shek has set up off Shanghai. And I've heard stories you're an old ex-pirate. You want to go talk to Isbrandtsen?"

I went to see old Hans Isbrandtsen and he asked me, "How much do you know about running a blockade?"

I said, "About everything there is to know. I used to be a smuggler."

"It'll take some doing," he said. "I'll make you chief mate on this run. You learn the ropes the way I want them learned and I'll put you on the next trip as skipper."

That was all right with me. I told him, "I have to get out of town for a while. And running the Chinese blockade past Chiang's navy into Shanghai seems to be the best offer I've had."

It would also be a large wad of dough for making the run. Provided we got back.

"Well, she's sailing tomorrow morning," Isbrandtsen said.

I called Sandy and I said, "Say, Sandy, I'm going to China. Tomorrow. I just signed on as chief mate."

Sandy said, "My God! I just found out this morning I'm pregnant."

I said, "Oh, my God. I'll be out four or five months. It's a long run."

I didn't tell her our exact port of call. I think she guessed it was something to do with that tomato-paste fiasco. China at that moment was really the best place for me to be—that far away from any of the guys involved.

My whole situation was ambiguous, because I had been an officer of the Black Diamond Line and a lot of the people on the docks had figured me as a spy for the company, anyway. And the tomato-paste job was big—it was worth maybe half a million dollars.

I took the deal to China. Of course, the situation there was nothing but trouble. Communist forces in China had driven Chiang out of Shanghai and Chiang had taken the position, "If I can't have Shanghai, neither can the Reds."

He took one of the destroyers America had given him and put it athwart the Yangtze River and kept everybody out. One British ship tried to get past and he sank her. One vessel of another flag also was fired on and sunk. So old Hans Isbrandtsen decided he would have a go at it.

Actually, we went in with two ships—the *Flying Clipper,* on which I was chief mate, and her sister ship, the *Flying Independence.* The plan was to go in from different angles—that way, one or the other had a good chance of getting through. Shanghai officials arranged to send us a river pilot. Chiang had changed all the markers in the river, and we had to have a pilot who knew the channels to get us through.

When we approached the river mouth, there was Chiang's American-built destroyer sitting there waiting for one of these two big freighters to try to make the run. The way their guns kept swinging around, from one ship to the other, they were obviously uncertain which one of us to shoot up first.

We watched the guns moving back and forth. Then they fired at the *Flying Independence*. When the warning shot whizzed across her bow, she promptly dropped her anchor.

We kept right on going, heading straight for that destroyer, which was sitting there smack in the middle of the channel. The pilot said to the old man, "Captain, you'd better start hauling off. You can go a good two destroyer lengths astern of her. You don't have to come this close."

I heard a loud horn blowing and something that sounded like shots. The Captain apparently didn't hear the pilot's words above the racket.

The pilot turned to me. He was an Australian, an old-time Yangtze River pilot. He and I'd been doing a lot of drinking in my cabin at night, yakking it up. To me this was all sport; this was like old times. I was breaking away for the first time in fourteen years and this was hilarious, the whole business. This was adventure.

Well, this pilot looked at me and said, "Hey, Jake. These Chinese are going to panic and start shooting if we don't change course now. In just about twenty seconds."

I said, "Christ, yes."

So I gave the order to change course so we would go under the stern of the destroyer and not run smack into her amidship or get shot the hell out of the water at point-blank range by a U.S.-built tin can bristling with five-inch guns.

But as we swung around her stern and started into the inner harbor—and all of us just waiting for the goddam

234

destroyer to open up on us—I saw something impossible happening on the destroyer itself. The men at the guns who supposedly should have been shooting at us were bringing those guns straight up, so they were pointing 90 degrees straight up at the sky.

We cleared the destroyer with very little to spare. I kept watching those guns pointing up at the sky and trying to reason out what the hell was going on. Nobody fired— not at us. Not one fucking shell.

Then, as I looked back, I saw something else: the destroyer was weighing anchor. It moved forward slowly and began to follow us in. Something had happened on board that ship—I knew they weren't taking us in as a captive vessel. If they were doing that, they would have kept the guns on us every instant.

The *Flying Independence* raised anchor and followed us in.

Not until the next day—after we were tied up and unloading—did I learn what had occurred in those few moments when we ran the blockade. What happened in those brief moments was a little-known, unsung Communist massacre on the destroyer.

Although the vessel was manned by officers supposedly loyal to Chiang, a small percentage of the crew were underground supporters of the Chinese Reds and were only waiting for the opportunity to take over. The arrival of the two Isbrandtsen ships—who legally had every right to engage in commerce with the Shanghai merchants if they could get inside the blockade—apparently appealed to the anti-Chiang forces on board the destroyer as the moment for a mutiny of international proportions.

The Red crewmen had brought out hidden knives and guns and murdered the ship's officers in a bloodbath that took place mainly on the bridge. They took over the vessel in the name of the Chinese Red government.

That was only the beginning of the slaughter on that ship. The next morning I was standing at the rail looking at the destroyer—tied up at the wharf—and I was watching and saw this bunch of Chinese going on board the destroyer with some black boxes. I thought, "They're going to shore up that destroyer, maybe to scrape the bottom or repaint."

It was a whole bunch of big black boxes. Somebody nearby said, "What have they got in those boxes—tea?"

I said it had to be something like that.

But the next instant I heard machine-gun fire. I ran to the bow and, Holy Jesus, they had about half their own crew or better lined up and they mowed them down on the destroyer deck, all of these crewmen who were loyal or suspected of being loyal to Chiang Kai-shek. That whole deck of that destroyer ran red with bodies and blood.

It was a mass slaughter—and efficiently done. I don't believe it was even reported in the press. The Red executioners stuffed the bodies into the black boxes, which we now realized were coffins brought there for this specific purpose, and carried them off for ultimate disposal. As far as I know, that destroyer is still serving the purposes not of American liberty but of law and order—Red Chinese style.

We were the first vessel in there in six months. They had had virtually no exports or imports in that period. Nobody knew what he was doing, either; the port managers and authorities and harbor officials were in a condition of almost total disorganization.

However, they were anxious for our cargo, and our main task was to get unloaded, reload with Chinese exports, and get out of there, all as quickly as possible.

This became my responsibility—the unloading, which we accomplished in two days, and the loading, which took seven. In those nine days I had exactly nine hours' sleep. It was a hell of a job. This was a big ship and we were taking on a really tremendous amount of Chinese cargo. I had to watch the loading day and night, because we had to keep the vessel on a perfectly even keel at all times.

I can't recall all the items we loaded. The list ran into the hundreds on the manifest. One of the major items was tea. We put on board four thousand *tons* of the stuff. That may not have been all the tea in China. But they tell me it was the largest shipment of its kind in the whole history of ocean sailing. It totalled eighty thousand cartons of tea.

Meanwhile, back in Greenpoint, Brooklyn, nobody ever did find out who stole that barge or its load of tomato paste. Things had been so hectic on the docks all those months, and even more so on the trip to China, I never did get around to collecting my bet of a case of whiskey from my stevedore pal Andy.

## 29. Sunday Afternoon

The world changes. People change.

My adventurous years changed, like everything else. My relationship with the Hemingways, especially with Hank and Patsy, changed also—but did not die. We had known each other, had lived through turbulence of many varieties, over a period of almost two decades.

In the closing years of the 1940s, Hank purchased a home out in Port Washington, Long Island. He was working hard at his editing and writing; he still had big dreams and big plans, some of them full of hints of the old adventures we had started out to follow—sailing the seven seas in some schooner or yawl or homemade yacht.

Sandy and I had not yet purchased our home in Sea Cliff, a few miles east of Port Washington. We were still living in Manhattan. On Sundays, however, in the spring and summer especially, Hank would have Sandy and me out there for the day, to visit with him and his wife.

Sandy remembers that period vividly and she wrote out a few paragraphs that hit the mark about what that time was like. (Sandy has always been a damned good reporter, especially when she was working for me on that paper in Brooklyn Heights.)

This is the way Sandy remembered and put it down:

"For those Sundays beginning in the Spring of 1947, we really became a part of Long Island suburbia. Not that you object, really. One finds a certain release. . . .

"We went out there a number of Sundays beginning in that Spring before Jake went back to sea with the Black Diamond Line and the Hemingways—Hank and Patsy—took off for other parts.

"We used to go by train, often with Peter Vest, who had been best man at our wedding (and a good friend of Hank's and his lovely wife), and our own two boys, Jon, who was five, and Mark, who was then about fourteen months old.

"Hank would meet us at the station in a battered second-hand car—don't remember the make—playing jovial host to the city folks. 'Glad to see you guys. Lots of fine food and drink waiting for us.'

"That was the way Hank would greet us. And the food was always good and the drink was always a couple of gallon jugs of inky red-eye wine—the kind Jake says always makes you mean as hell. Actually he says it brings out the worst or best of what you are.

"We would all crowd into the car—and it really meant crowd—because Hank's two boys, Jake and Peter, who were about seven and nine then, would come along to meet us. The mood was always one of people determined to have

239

a good time. Sunday in the country for the city people and a chance for Hank and Patsy to share the rich suburban life with us.

"The house was a three-bedroom white frame house, with a glassed-in sun porch across the front. The porch was where the kids' gear was kept and where the puppy dog, who at first wasn't housebroken, was confined. The house itself was sparsely furnished, without rugs, although the boys' rooms were complete with lots of sporting equipment and books and toys.

"It was a genuine effort to provide the boys with a mother, a father, a nice home in the suburbs with a big yard, and as many of the material things as they needed to feel secure. The house was bought on the GI Bill, and neither Jake nor I can remember how long they lived there.

"After we arrived at the house we would sit around and talk through, around, over and about the kids and start on the wine while Patsy got dinner ready. I think those dinners must have stretched their budget, because, while they weren't fancy, there was always plenty and to spare for everybody.

"After dinner was cleared away, the kids would play in the yard and then we would all go down to the marina in Port Washington Harbor where Hank kept his sailing dinghy and we'd take turns going out on it. It's the kind of thing you do for your city-bound friends.

"After a couple of hours of that we would go back to the house and finish up the wine. Patsy would begin to sulk, Hank would begin to torture Patsy, the kids would get fretful, and it would be time to go. But we always went back the next time because Jake was genuinely fond of Hank and Patsy, and the children seemed to enjoy themselves. They liked the train ride, anyway.

"If one wanted to highlight any special item, I guess it might be how strange, or even ridiculous, it was for Jake and Hank to be out sailing in a dinghy in Port Washington Harbor on a suburban Sunday afternoon. That and the really earnest attempt of the Hank Hemingways to set down 'roots' for their kids.

"I think they really wanted to sell us on that type of life in the suburbs, the way married people always like to marry off their bachelor friends. But at the time we thought suburbia was for the birds and found it somewhat sad and unnecessary.

"It was seven years, and two additional kids later, before we succumbed and bought a home for ourselves in Sea Cliff, a lovely old suburban town of white-framed houses only a few miles east of Port Washington on Long Island's north shore."

That was how Sandy remembered it. We did talk about a lot of things those afternoons, sitting around on the porch drinking red wine, fooling around in that dinghy out on the water.

We talked about ourselves and the families and the kids and what they were learning or not learning. We talked about the big ideas we had or used to have.

Sometimes we would talk about Stein and where he was and what he was doing or writing and had just finished. We heard he was working on a book about an old man, a sea story of some kind. It was in the hands of his pub-

241

lishers. I recall wondering: Was it Stein himself—Papa Hemingway—looking into the shadows ahead?

Hank himself was writing his own first novel, *The Sound of the Trumpet*. He autographed a copy for me when it was published. The inscription read:

> "This book is for Jake Klimo, who will have his own damn fabulous words to beat it whenever he wants to. Because I know he has the stuff—
>
> > With affection—
> >
> > > Les Hemingway"

It was dated December 1, 1953. The book itself was dedicated to Hank's two sons, Jake and Peter.

its own decision; there can be no definitive answer. He was not well physically or mentally; for months he had been in the Mayo Clinic and under heavy sedation and medical care; he had had considerable shock treatment and psychotherapy.

Stein was a goddam good fighter all his life, writing or not writing, fishing, boxing, screwing, drinking—he was a great fighter and a hard loser.

I've thought about this a hell of a lot, because whatever anyone else may believe or even deny, this man Stein and I were friends and you couldn't help but admire him and respect him. And thank him. A son-of-a-bitch at times, a tormented soul. But a great man; a great man and a great writer.

I believe this last aspect—his role as a writer—is the thing that did it, that drove him to write finis to his life. It was not merely the physical or psychological assault going on within him; it was also because he could not write any more, because he no longer had the strength or freedom from those other tormenting concerns to put it all down.

He was the old lion, the great old lion, or the weary bull, the dying bull, lacking the strength to challenge the glittering sword. But he knew it all so well, the details of it all so well. He was quite able to do it for himself, quietly and skillfully and without the least chance of missing his mark, or lingering one moment beyond the allotted time.

I find myself wondering—could it possibly have been that this was his way of telling his last story? Could the whole thing, the whole event, the whole experience, be a fragment out of the one story he could never put down—but the ending of which he wrote in his own special way?

244

Maybe this was the enigmatic finish he left to us deliberately, a final episode told not with pen or pencil but with the blast of a shotgun in the Sunday morning quiet.

Brutal, yes. Brutal and swift. But not an untypical Hemingway ending, anyway you want to take it.